French - Russian

# LEARNING FLASHCARDS

## FOR BABIES TODDLERS

# alligator

аллигатор

The alligator is having a party.

# fourmi

муравей

The ant is red.

# ours

медведь

The bear loves you.

# abeille

пчела

The bee is saying hello.

# oiseau

птица

The bird is flying.

# papillon

бабочка

The butterfly is pretty.

# chameau

верблюд

The camel has a hump.

# chat

кошка

The cat is happy.

# dinosaure

динозавр

The dinosaur is laying eggs.

# poulet

курица

The chicken is dancing.

# vache

корова

The cow has a bell.

# cerf

олень

The reindeer has a toy.

# chien

собака

The dog has two floppy ears.

# dauphin

дельфин

The dolphin is swimming.

# canard

утка

The duck has a bow.

# aigle

орел

The eagle is looking for food.

# l'éléphant

слон

The elephant is sitting.

# poisson

рыбы

The fish is a clownfish.

# libellule

стрекоза

The dragonfly is blue.

# renard

лиса

The fox has a red nose.

# grenouille

лягушка

The frog is smiling.

# girafe

жирафа

The giraffe has a long neck.

# chèvre

козел

The goat has a beard

# ver de terre

червь

The worm is in the apple

# poule

курица

The hen has chicks.

# hippopotame

бегемот

The hippo is big.

# cheval

лошадь

The horse is fast.

# kangourou

кенгуру

The kangaroo has a baby.

# chaton

котенок

The kitten is playing.

# lion

лев

The lion has a mane.

# homard

омар

The lobster is red.

# singe

обезьяна

The monkey has a tail.

# poulpe

осьминог

The octopus has food.

# hibou

сова

The owls have big eyes.

# panda

панда

The panda wears a diaper.

# porc

свинья

The pig is fat and pink.

# chiot

щенок

The dog is brown.

# lapin

кролик

The rabbit has a carrot.

# rat

крыса

The mouse is writing something.

# crabe

краб

The crab has two pinchers.

# requin

акула

The shark is scary.

# mouton

овец

The sheep are very fluffy.

# escargot

улитка

The snail is slow.

# serpent

змея

The snake has poison.

# araignée

паук

The spider is purple.

# écureuil

белка

The squirrel has a nut.

# tigre

тигр

The tiger has a red bow.

# tortue

черепаха

The turtle has a shell.

# loup

волк

The wolf is smiling.

# zèbre

зебра

The zebra is black and white.

# dinde

турция

The turkey has two legs.

# coq

петух

The rooster will crow.

# perroquet

попугай

The parrot is colorful.

# hérisson

еж

The hedgehog has apples.

# pomme

яблоко

The apple has a leaf.

# abricot

абрикос

The apricot is yellow.

# avocat

авокадо

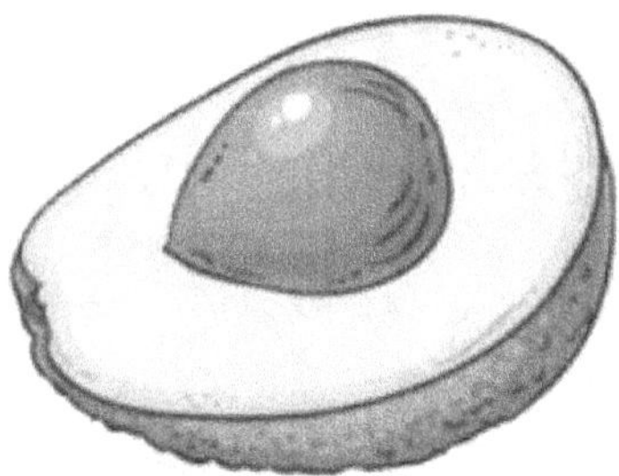

The avocado has a nut.

# banane

банан

The banana is yellow.

# la mûre

ежевика

There are a lot of blackberries.

# cassis

черная смородина

The blackcurrants are yummy.

# myrtille

черника

The blueberries are sweet.

# cerise

вишня

The cherries have a stem.

# noix de coco

кокос

The coconuts have juice.

# figues

инжир

The fig has seeds.

# grain de raisin

виноград

The grapes are purple.

# pamplemousse

грейпфрут

The grapefruits are sour.

# kiwi

киви

The kiwi is fresh.

# citron

лимон

The lemons are yellow.

# citron vert

лайм

We have lots of lime.

# litchi

нефелиум

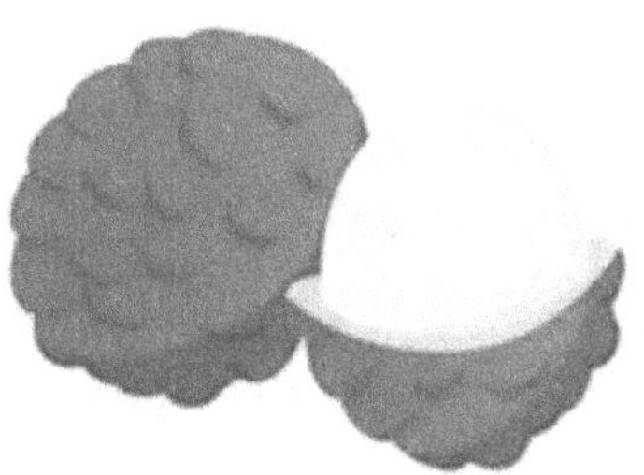

I like to eat lychee.

# mandarine

мандарин

Oranges are refreshing.

# mangue

манго

Mango is my favorite fruit.

# orange

оранжевый

Mandarins are like oranges.

# papaye

папайя

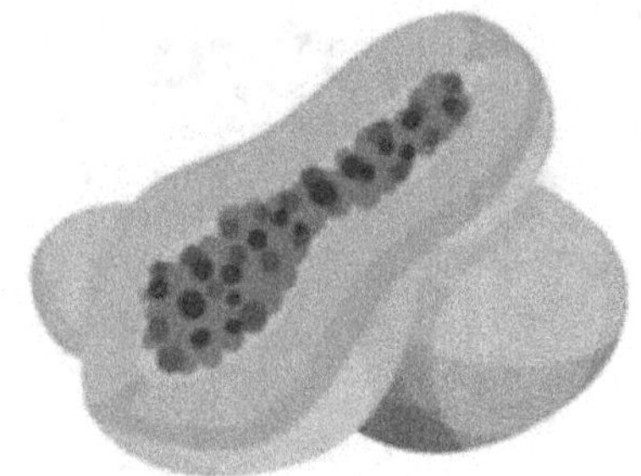

Papayas have lots of seeds.

# pêche

персик

Peaches are juicy.

# poire

груша

Pears have a strange figure.

# ananas

ананас

The pineapple has a thumbs up.

# prune

слива

Plums are healthy for you.

# grenade

гранатовый

Pomegranates are all red.

# framboise

малина

The raspberry is shiny.

# fraise

клубника

The strawberry has leaves on top.

# pastèque

арбуз

The watermelon is big.

# mandarine

мандарин

The tangerine looks like an orange.

# tarte

пирог

I like to eat apple pie.

## gâteau

торт

That cake is huge.

## bonbons

конфеты

Candy is not good for your teeth.

## biscuit

печенье

Cookies are easy to make.

## donut

пончик

I like strawberry donuts.

## crème glacée

мороженое

The ice cream is melting.

## muffin

оладья

The muffin has a cute wrapper.

# pudding

пудинг

We eat pudding on Christmas.

# classeur

связующее вещество

I keep pictures in my binder.

# livre

книга

I like to eat books.

# sac à dos

рюкзак

The backpack has lots of stuff.

# les ciseaux

ножницы

I have scissors in my bag.

# épingles

pins

Pins can hold stuff up.

# agrafe

клип

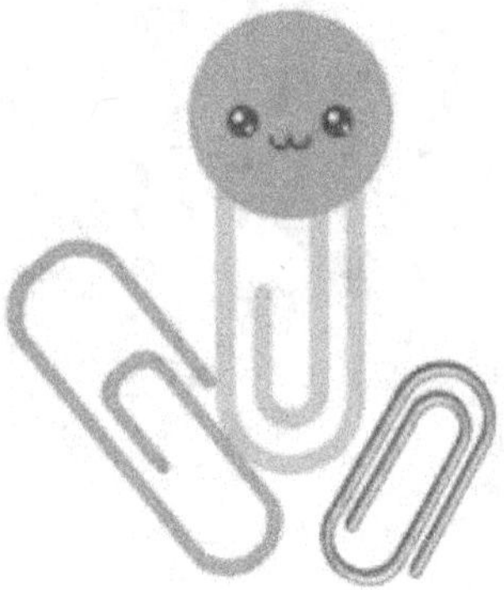

Clips can hold up paper.

# papier

бумага

I have lots of paper.

# agrafeuse

стэплер

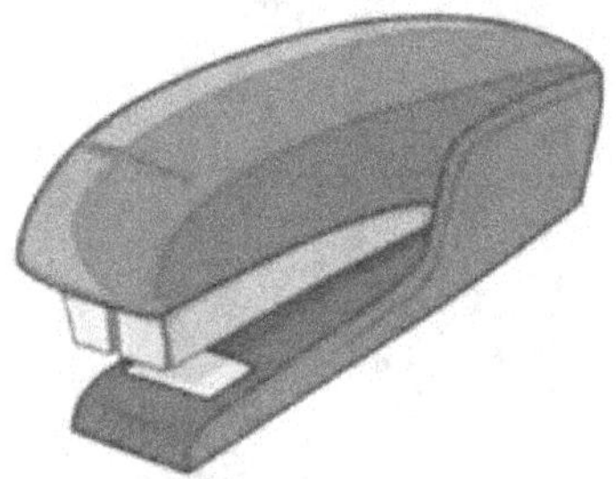

My stapler is shiny and red.

# calculatrice

калькулятор

My calculator has buttons.

# règle

линейка

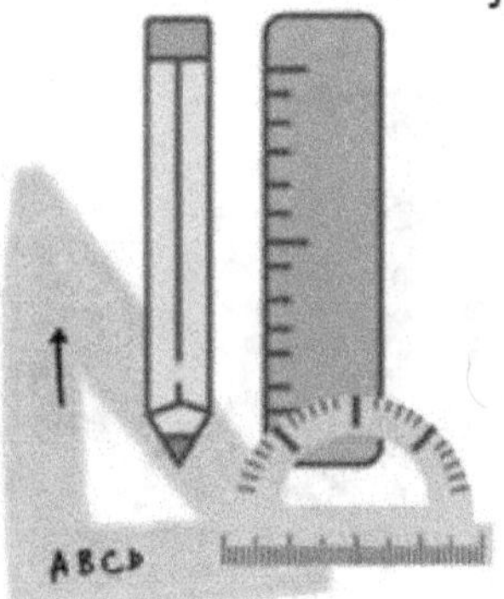


I have lots of rulers.

# la colle

клей

The glue is sticky.

# bibliothèque

книжный шкаф

My bookcase has lots of things.

# calendrier

календарь

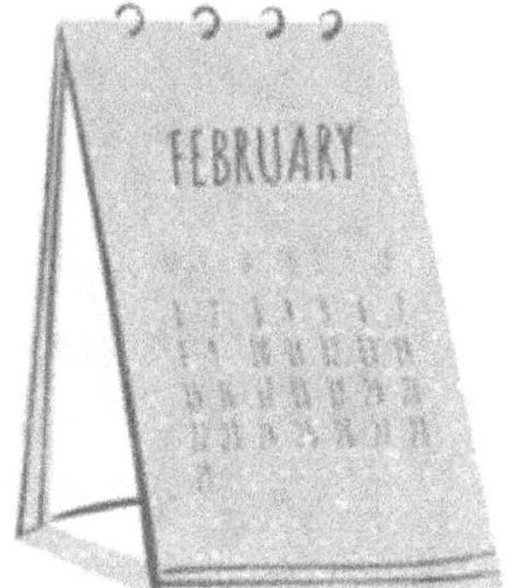


I have a calendar on my table.

# chaise

стул

My chair is fancy.

# l'horloge

часы

The clock says that it's 3 o'clock.

# ordinateur

компьютер

I do things on my computer.

# bureaux

парты

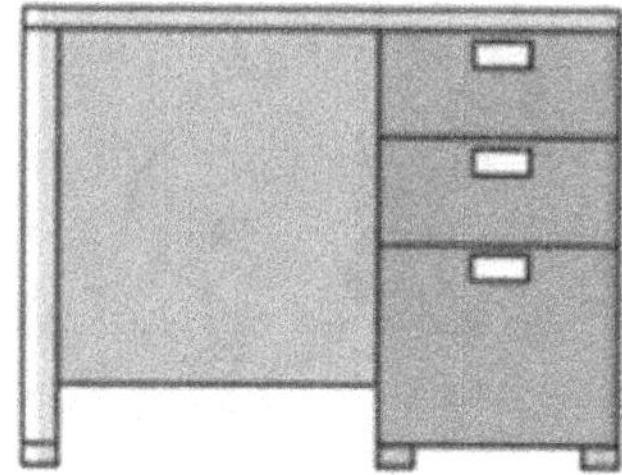

I put lots of things on my desk.

# dictionnaire

словарь

The dictionary has lots of words.

# la gomme

ластик

Erasers are used with pencils.

# carte

карта

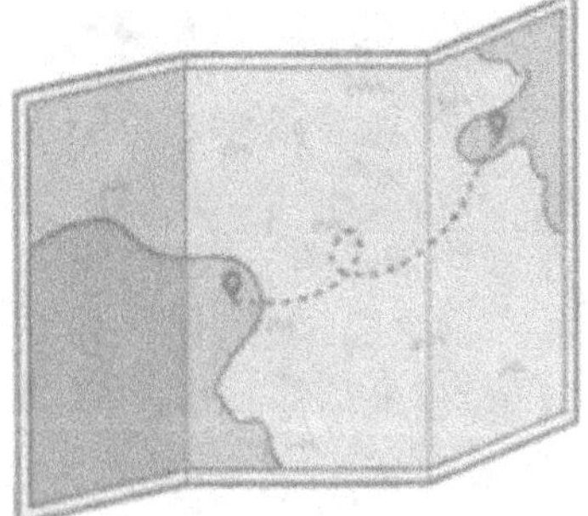

The map shows you different places.

# carnet

ноутбук

I use notebooks at school.

# stylo

ручка

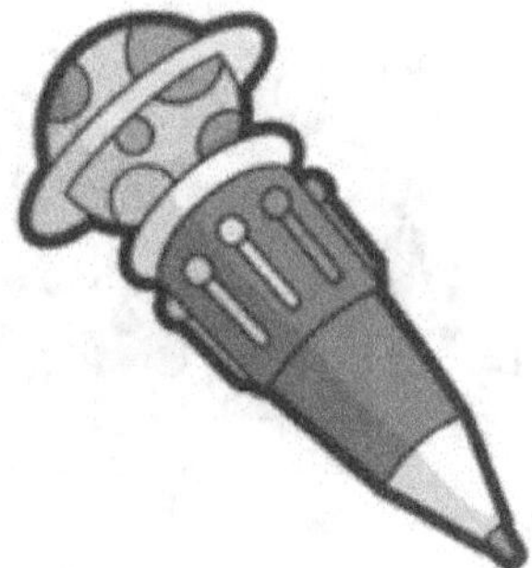

My pen is very pretty.

# crayon

карандаш

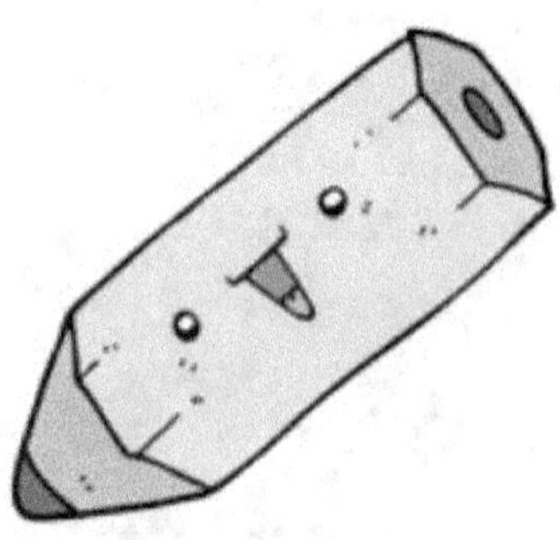

My friend gave me a pencil.

# ceinture

ремень

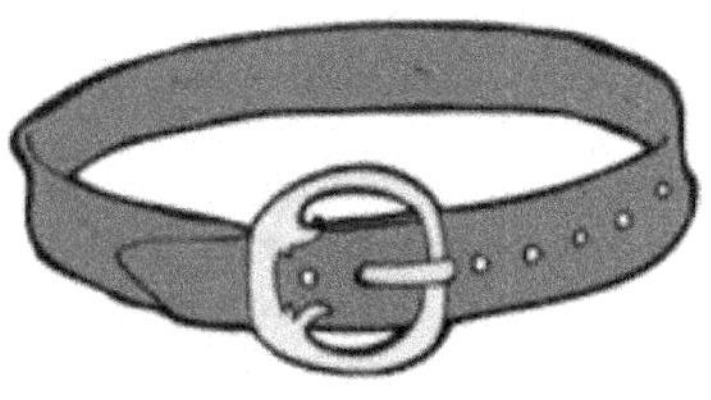

I have a belt on my pants.

# bottes

ботинки

I have big brown boots.

# chapeau

шляпа

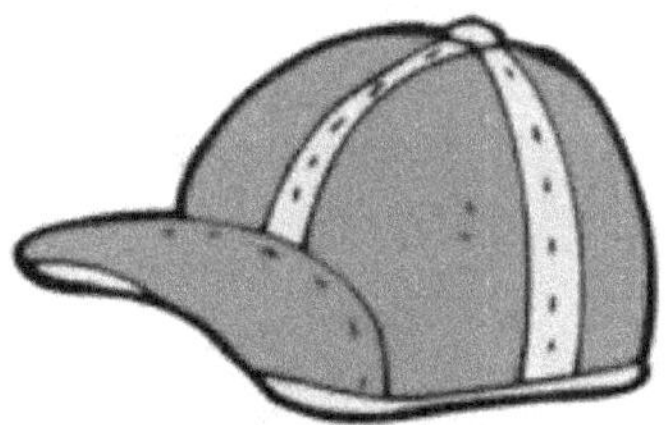

My mom bought me a new cap.

# manteau

пальто

She has a long yellow coat.

# robes

платья

My dress has a bow.

# gants

перчатки

I got new gloves.

# chapeau

шляпа

That hat is for a wicked witch.

# veste

куртка

The jacket is cozy.

# jeans

джинсы

My jeans are long.

# pyjamas

пижама

I sleep in my pajamas.

# un pantalon

штаны

The bear is wearing pants.

# imperméable

плащ

We wear our raincoats when it is raining.

# écharpe

шарф

The baby has a scarf around his neck.

# chemise

рубашка

I like this shirt the best.

# des chaussures

туфли

I have red and blue shoes.

# jupe

юбка

My skirt has lots of buttons.

# pantalon

широкие брюки

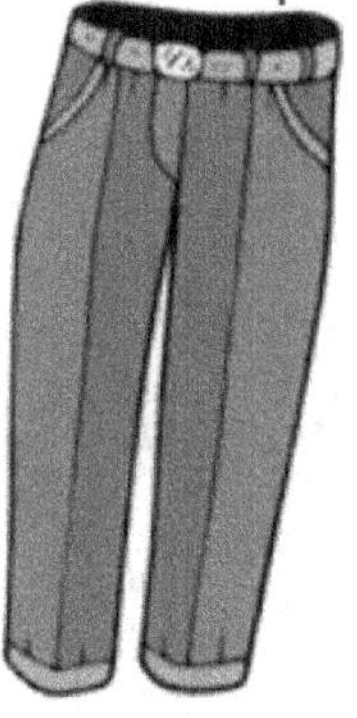

My dad wears slacks.

# chaussons

домашняя обувь

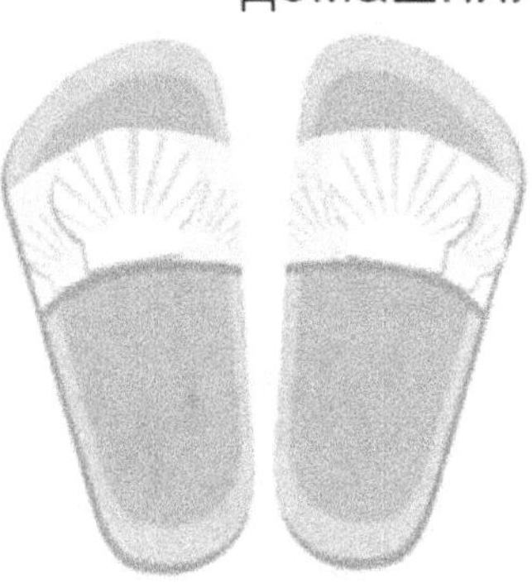

I have seashells on my sandals.

# chaussettes

носки

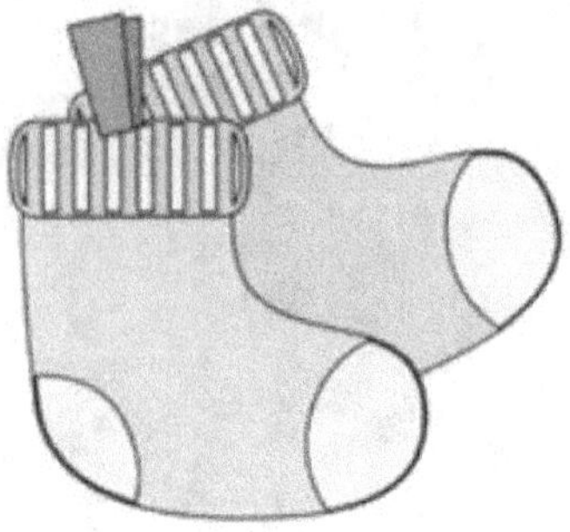

My baby sister wears socks.

# costume

подходить

My brother is wearing a suit.

# chandail

свитер

I am wearing a sweater for winter.

# cravate

галстук

My dad wears a tie to meetings.

# pantalon

штаны

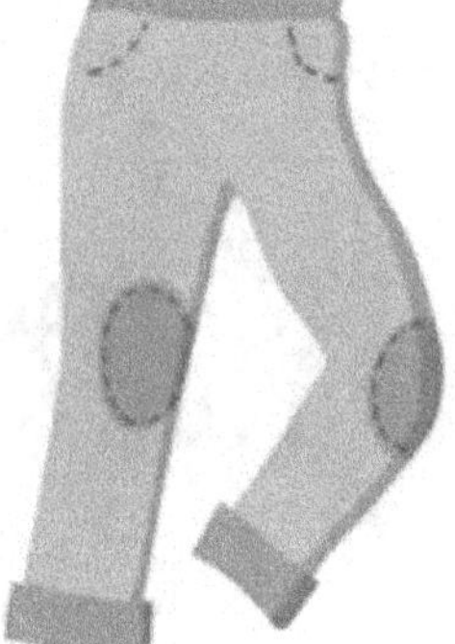

The trousers look like jeans.

# slip

трусы

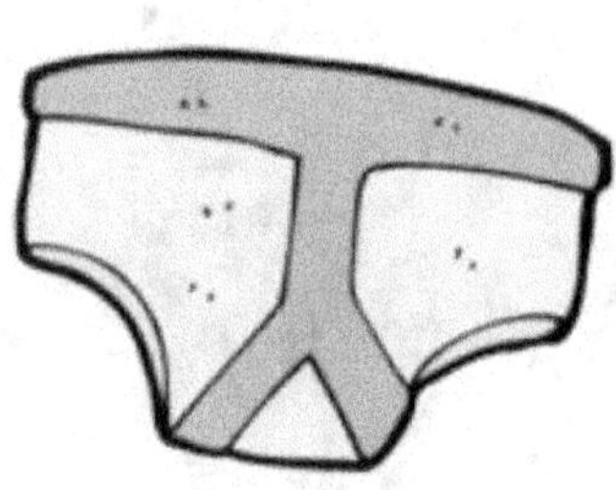

I always wear my underwear.

# maillot de corps

нижняя рубаха

My undershirt has a star.

# une

один

Number one and the bee are friends.

# deux

два

The cat and the mouse both love two.

# trois

три

The bear gives number three a present.

# quatre

четыре

Number four is a home for the cat.

# cinq

пять

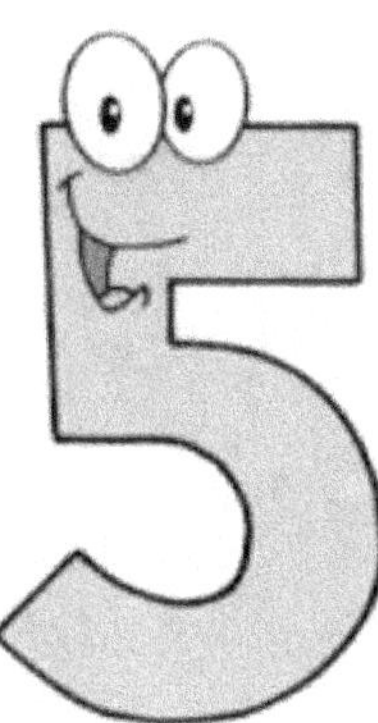

Number five hatches an egg.

# six

шесть

Number six is going to eat a carrot.

# sept

семь

Number seven is playing with the tiger.

# huit

восемь

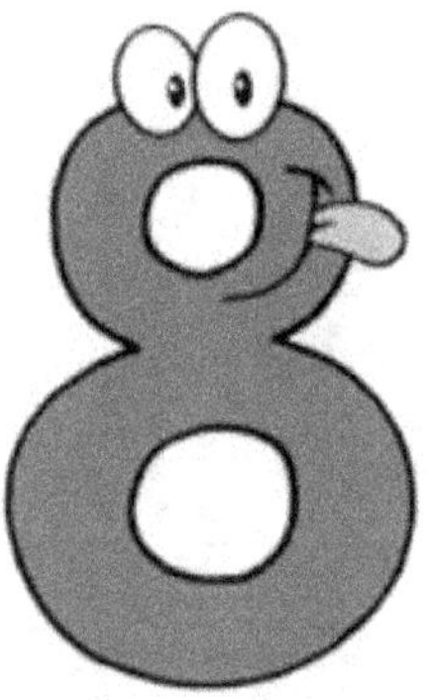

Number eight is funny.

# neuf

девять

Number nine meets the parrot.

# dix

десять

Number ten is smiling.

# onze

одиннадцать

Number eleven has big eyes.

# douze

двенадцать

Number twelve is number one and two.

# treize

13

Number thirteen is excited.

# quatorze

14

The number fourteen is vast.

# quinze

15

The number fifteen is green.

# seize

шестнадцать

Sixteen is my lucky number.

# dix-sept

семнадцать

Number seventeen look alike.

# dix-huit

восемнадцать

Number eighteen will go to the circus.

# dix-neuf

19

I am nineteen now!

# vingt

20

Number twenty has a zero.

# fourmi

муравей

The ant has lots of legs.

# cloche

колокол

The bell will ring.

# vache

корова

The cow has a bow.

# poupée

кукла

She has a cute bear doll.

# oeuf

яйцо

The chick has hatched out of the egg.

# poisson

рыбы

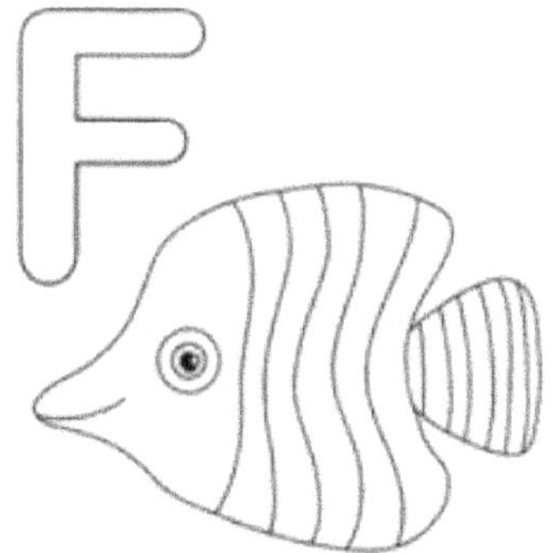

The fish is swimming in the water.

# chèvre

козел

The goat is sitting on the grass.

# chapeau

шляпа

He is wearing a hat.

# crème glacée

мороженое

I like to eat ice cream.

# confiture

варенье

The kitten is sitting on the jam jar.

# chaton

котенок

The cat is sleeping on the floor.

# lion

лев

The lion is waiting for the tiger.

# rat

крыса

The mouse has lots of presents.

# nez

нос

The reindeer has a red nose.

# hibou

сова

The owl is sleeping.

# porc

свинья

The pig will eat cupcakes.

# reine

королева

The queen has a big crown.

# lapin

кролик

The rabbit is jumping up and down.

# mouton

овец

The sheep have fluffy wool.

# tortue

черепаха

The turtle has a shell.

# parapluie

зонтик

The mouse is holding an umbrella.

# van

фургон

The van is driving along the road.

# pastèque

арбуз

The watermelon has lots of seeds.

# xylophone

ксилофон

We are going to play the xylophone.

# yaourt

йогурт

We opened the yogurt can.

# zèbre

зебра

The zebra is surprised.

# rose

розовый

color the word and
the picture in pink

Most of my clothes are pink.

# marron

коричневый

color the word and
the picture in pink

brown

My chocolate is brown.

# gris

серый

color the word and
the picture in pink

gray

I don't like the color gray.

# vert

зеленый

color the word and
the picture in pink

green

The vegetables are green.

# jaune

желтый

color the word and
the picture in pink

yellow

Bananas are yellow.

# blanc

белый

color the word and
the picture in pink

white

The paper that I write on is white.

# rouge

красный

color the word and
the picture in pink

red

Apples are red.

# bleu

синий

color the word and
the picture in pink

The night sky is blue.

# percer

дрель

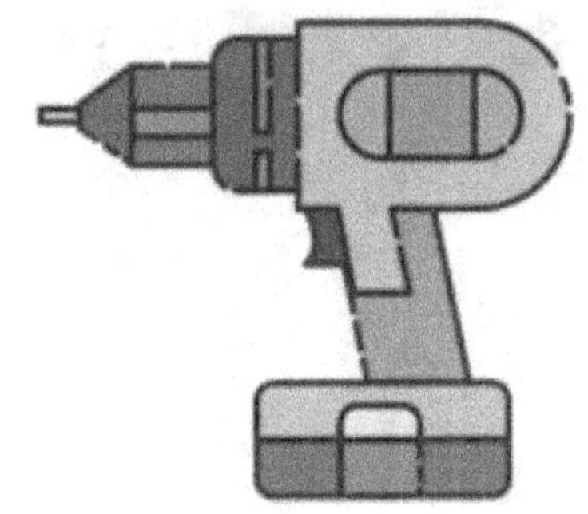

The drill will help us fix this.

# marteau

молоток

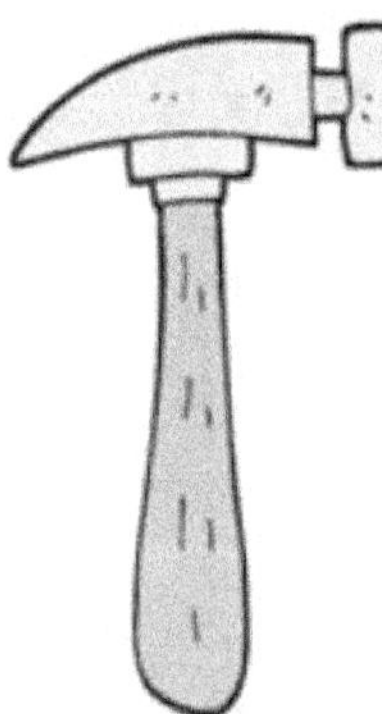

The hammer is going to nail the picture.

# couteau

нож

The knife is sharp.

# pinces

плоскогубцы

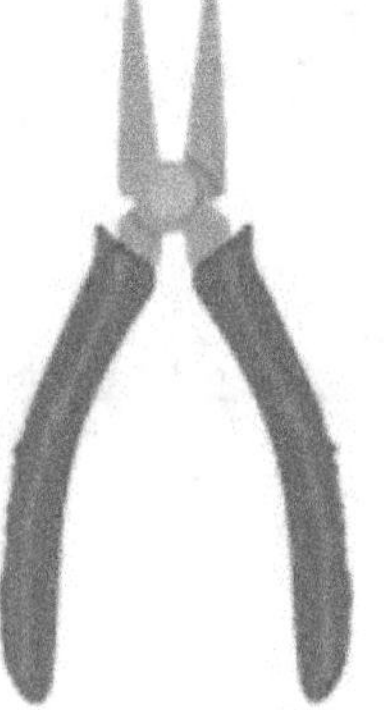

The plier is used for many things.

# vu

пила

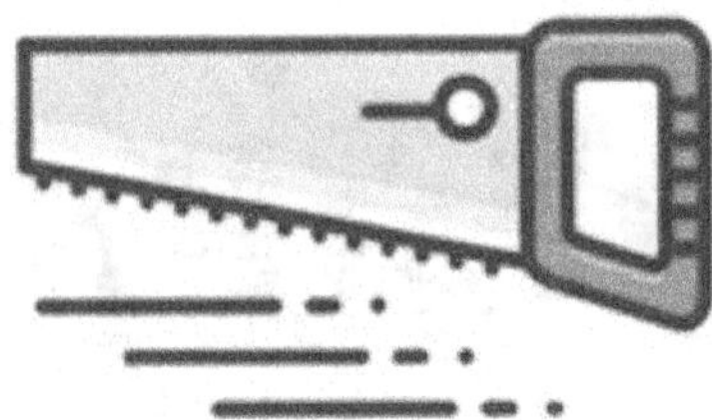

The saw can chop wood.

# les ciseaux

ножницы

I use scissors to cut paper.

# tournevis

отвертка

The screwdriver can screw in the knots.

# clé

гаечный ключ

The wrench can help unscrew the knots.

# avion

самолет

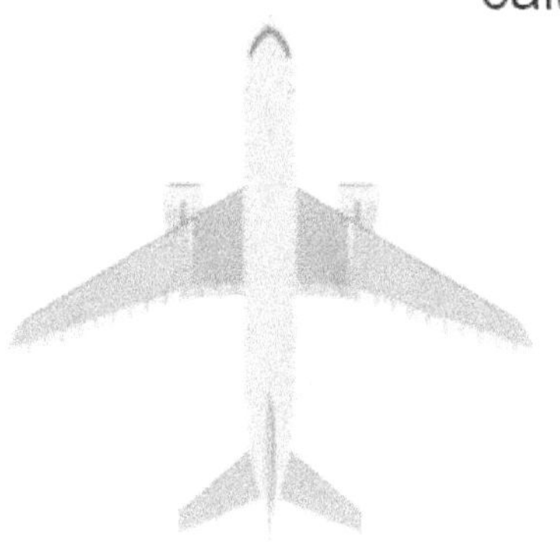

The airplane is going to leave now.

# vélo

велосипед

The bicycle is beautiful.

# bateau

лодка

The boat is floating on the water.

# autobus

автобус

The bus is going to school.

# voiture

машина

The car is green.

# hélicoptère

вертолет

The helicopter is looking for something.

# cheval

лошадь

You can ride the horse.

# jet

реактивный самолет

The jet is high-speed.

# moto

мотоцикл

The motorcycle is on the road.

# navire

корабль

The ship is on the water.

# métro

метро

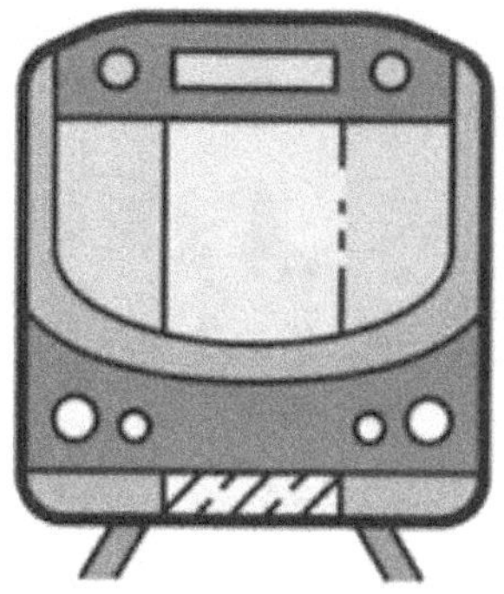

My mom goes on the subway to work.

# taxi

такси

The taxi has someone inside.

# train

поезд

The train is going slowly.

# un camion

грузовая машина

The truck has stuff in it.

# asperges

спаржа

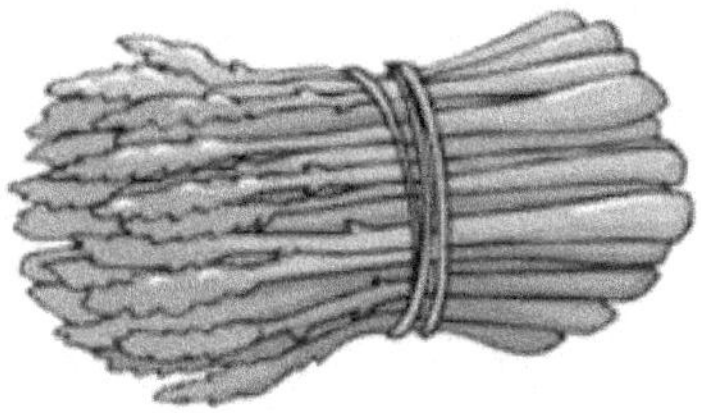

The asparagus is in a bundle.

# des haricots

фасоль

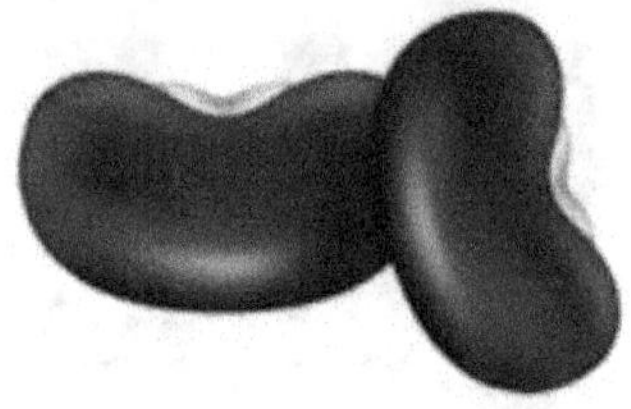

The beans are smooth.

# brocoli

брокколи

The broccoli is dancing.

# chou

капуста

Bunnies like to eat cabbage.

# carotte

морковь

The carrots are very long.

# céleri

сельдерей

The celery has lots of leaves.

# blé

кукуруза

Corn soup is delicious.

# concombre

огурец

The cucumbers are cut into pieces.

# aubergine

баклажан

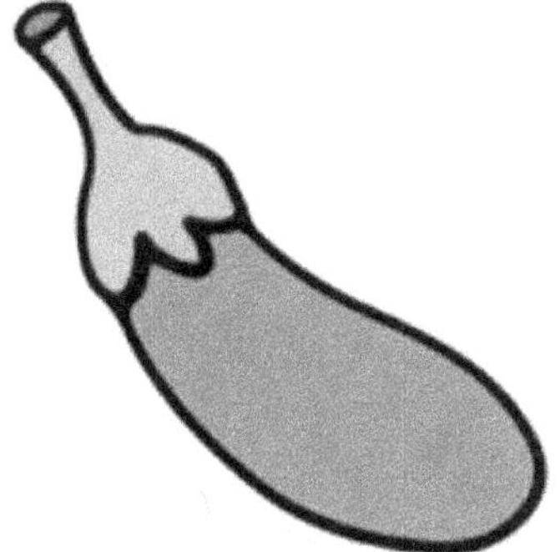

The eggplant is purple.

# poivre vert

зеленый перец

The green pepper is juicy.

# salade

салат

The lettuce is all green.

# oignon

лук

The onions make my eyes water.

# pois

горох

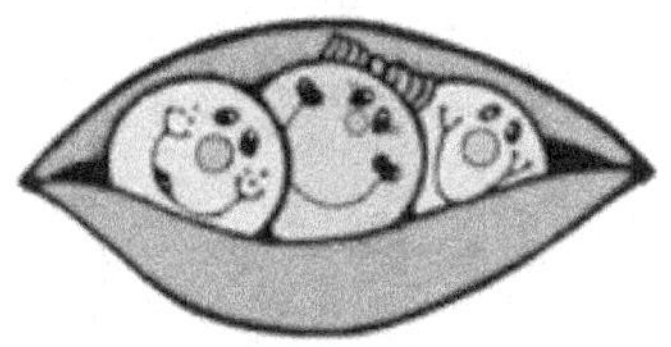

The peas are all in a pod.

# patate

картошка

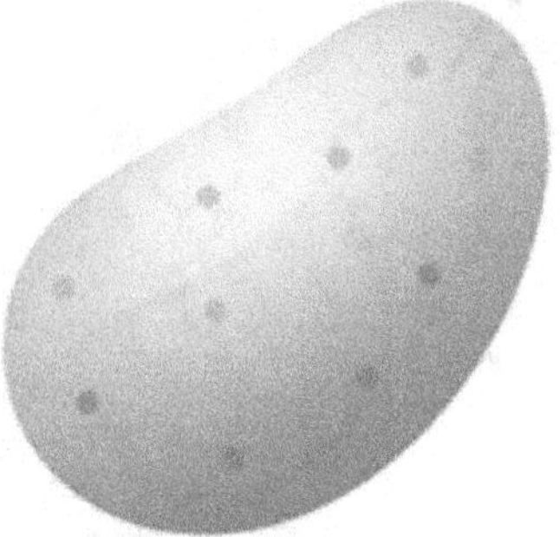

The potato is very shiny.

# citrouille

тыква

The pumpkin is for Halloween.

# un radis

редис

The radish is a type of vegetable.

# épinard

шпинат

The spinach is good with cheese.

# patate douce

сладкий картофель

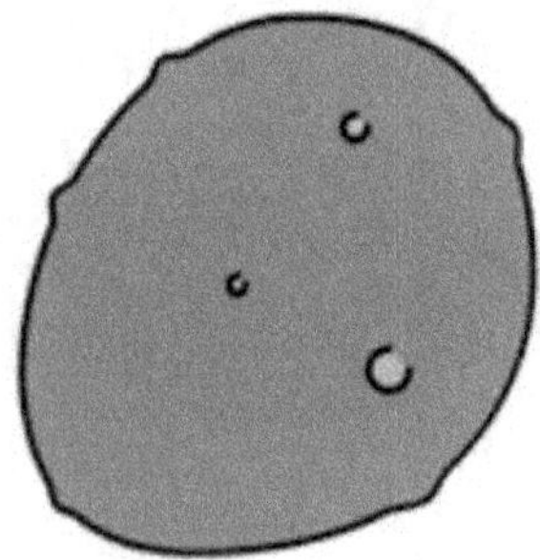

The sweet potato is quite sweet.

# tomate

помидор

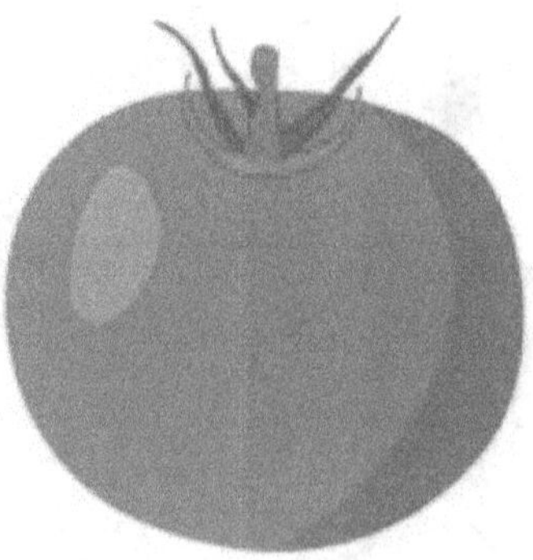

I don't like to eat tomatoes.

# navet

репа

My mom bought some turnips.

# nuageux

облачный

The weather is cloudy today.

# du froid

холодный

I like cold weather.

# cool

прохладный

The temperature is cold today.

# brumeux

туманный

The fog is so strong I can't see the city.

# chaud

горячий

The fire is burning hot.

# humide

влажный

It's so humid and wet today.

# pluvieux

дождливый

It's raining very hard.

# neigeux

снежный

Welcome to snow land!

# orageux

штормовой

I hate the stormy weather.

# ensoleillé

солнечно

The sun is shining!

# chaud

тёплый

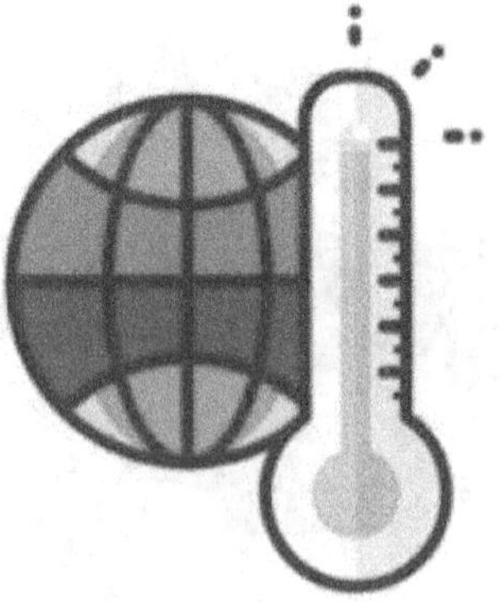

The whole world is warm today!

# venteux

ветреный

The leaves are blowing away since it's so windy!

# tante

тетка

My aunt is very nice to me.

# frère

брат

My brother is very fun to play with.

# cousin

двоюродная сестра

I love going to the playground with my cousin.

# fille

дочь

I like to read books with my daughter.

# père

отец

My father is playing with me.

# petite fille

внучка

My granddaughter has blond hair.

# grand-mère

бабушка

My grandmother is very old and has glasses.

# petit fils

внук

My grandson and I are very excited today!

# mère

мама

My mother likes to pick me up.

# neveu

племянник

My father's nephew is my cousin.

# nièce

племянница

My niece is very good at playing ball.

# sœur

сестра

My sister is so pretty!

# fils

сын

My son likes to play with toy cars.

# belle fille

падчерица

My stepdaughter likes the color orange.

# belle-mère

мачеха

My stepmother is pretty.

# beau-fils

пасынок

This is my stepson, Greg.

# oncle

дядя

My uncle tells lots of funny jokes.

# bol

миска

The bowl has nothing inside.

# tasse

кружка

My mom drinks her coffee out of a cup.

# plat

блюдо

That dish has a bone inside.

# fourchette

вилка

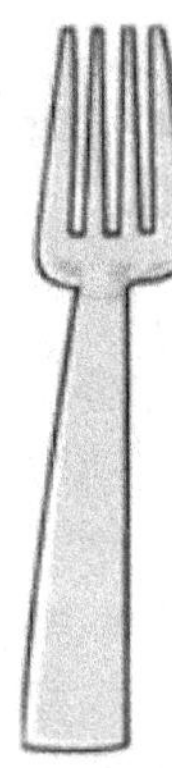

We have more spoons than forks.

# verre

стекло

I have a glass of water on my desk.

# couteau

нож

I have a knife in my kitchen.

# agresser

кружка

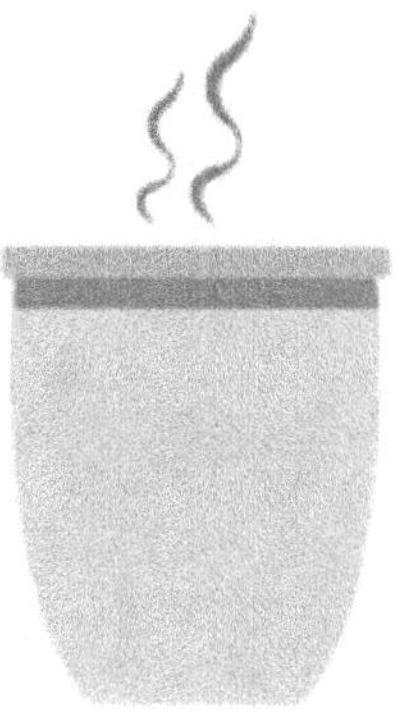

This mug of coffee is for my dad.

# serviette de table

салфетка

You can use the napkins to clean your hands.

# poivre

перец

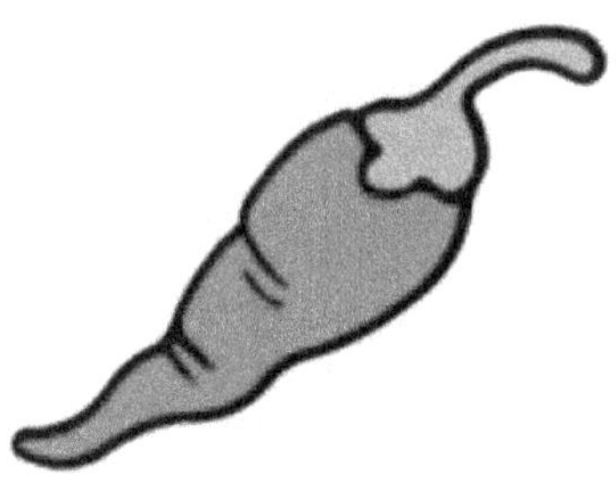

The pepper is very spicy.

# lanceur

кувшин

Pour yourself some lemonade from the pitcher.

# assiette

пластина

Can you help me wash the plates?

# salade

салат

The salad is very healthy for you.

# sel

поваренная соль

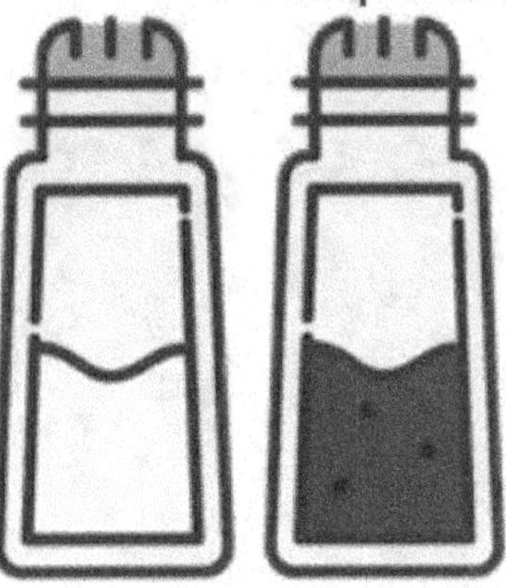

The salt tastes good with a few pinches of pepper.

# soucoupe

блюдце

The plate is for my cup.

# cuillère

ложка

I use a spoon to eat my rice.

# sucre

сахар

The pack of sugar is very heavy.

# dimanche

воскресенье

Sunday

Sunday is the day to go to Church!

# lundi

понедельник

Monday

Monday is the day to start school.

# mardi

вторник

Tuesday

We will go to the shops on Tuesday.

# mercredi

среда

Wednesday

Wednesday is hard to spell!

# jeudi

четверг

Thursday

Thursday is the fourth day of the week!

# vendredi

пятница

Friday

My birthday is on Friday!

# samedi

суббота

Saturday

Saturday is the weekend!

# cuire

выпекать

The chef will bake a cake.

# ébullition

кипятить

I will boil the eggs.

# griller

жариться

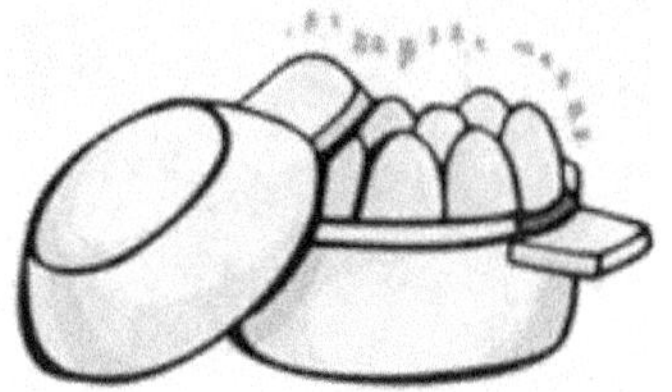

Broil is very yummy.

# ouvre-boîte

открывашка

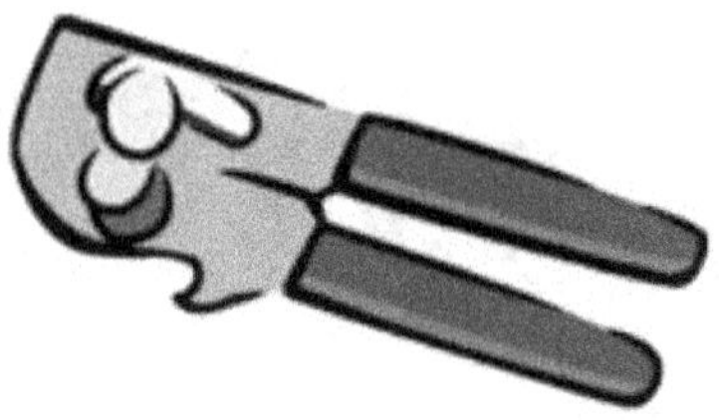

That can opener is used for opening cans.

# frire

жарить

The pan can fry lots of things.

# gril

гриль

We have a grill in our backyard.

# tasse à mesurer

мензурка

My mom uses the measuring cup for baking.

# cuillère à mesurer

мерная ложка

I use a measuring spoon to eat my dessert.

# four micro onde

микроволновая печь

The microwave is used to heat food.

# bol à mélanger

миска для смешивания

She is using the mixing bowl to mix things.

# serviettes en papier

бумажные полотенца

Dry your hands with paper towels.

# poché aux œufs

яйцо-пашот

The poach is put on noodles.

# porte pot

держатель для горшка

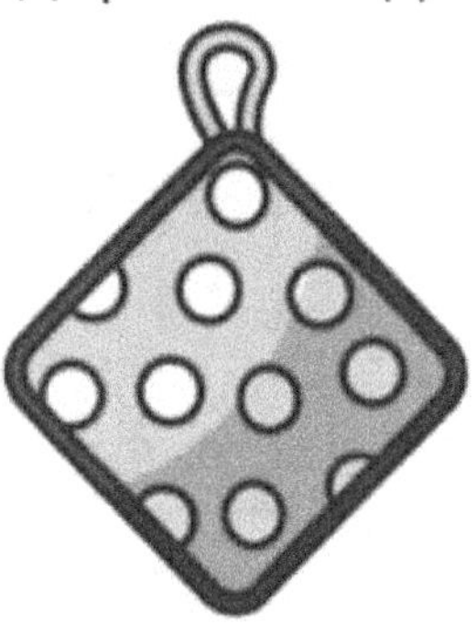

The potholder is soft.

# rôti

обжиг

The chef made roast chicken.

# rouleau à pâtisserie

скалка

He is holding a rolling pin.

# brouiller

свалка

My mom is making scrambled eggs for breakfast.

# mijoter

кипятить на медленном огне

The simmer is rice today.

# couteau

нож

The knife is sharp.

# cuillère

ложка

I eat my food with a spoon and fork.

# spatule

шпатель

The spatula will help us flip the steak over.

# vapeur

пар

The steam is coming from the pot.

# passoire

стяжка

The strainer is used to strain stuff.

# minuteur

таймер

I set my timer for 12:00.

# fourchette

вилка

I have lots of metallic forks.

# grille-pain

тостер

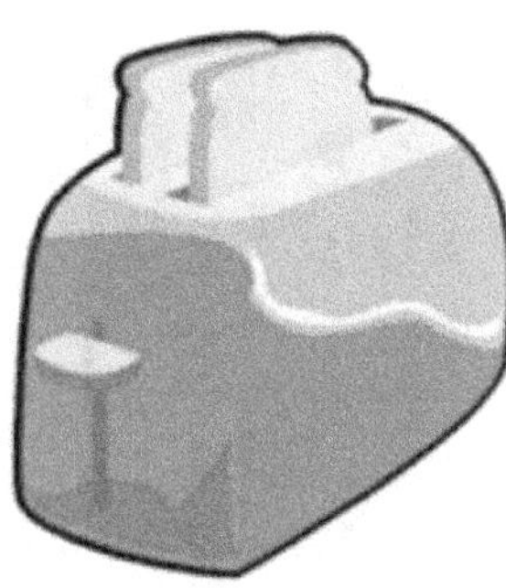

The toaster will toast my bread.

# bouilloire

чайник

The kettle has tea inside.

# réfrigérateur

холодильник

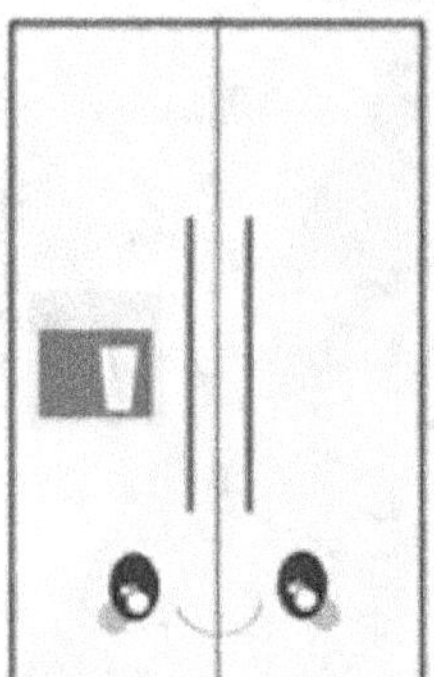

The refrigerator has lots of things inside.

# mixeur

смеситель

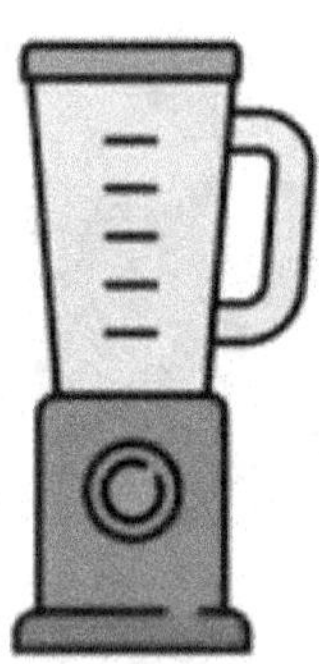

The blender will mix up my fruits.

# cabinets

шкафы

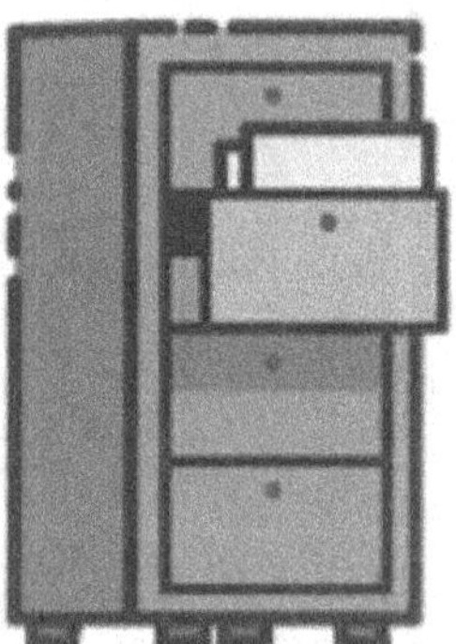

The cabinet has my paper inside.

# placard

чулан

The cupboard has lots of books.

# four micro onde

СВЧ

The microwave will heat my food.

# arrière

назад

She has a slender back.

# des joues

щеки

She kisses her mom on the cheek.

# poitrine

грудь

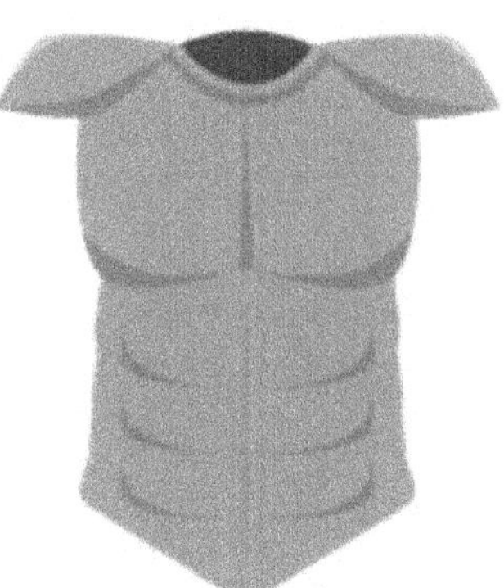

The armor is for your chest.

# menton

подбородок

This is my chin!

# oreilles

уши

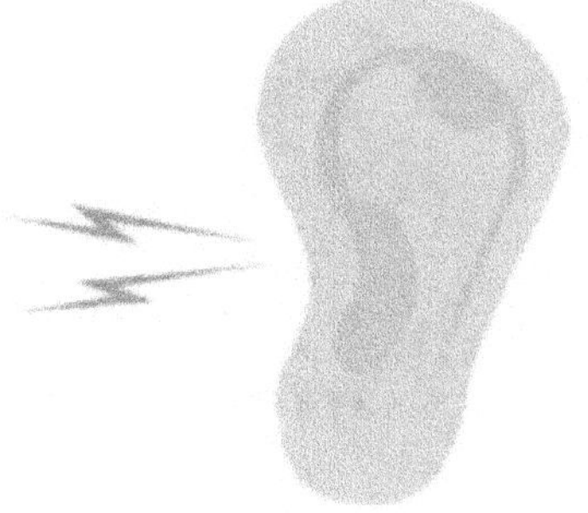

The ear is hearing something.

# les sourcils

брови

The eyebrows are raised.

# yeux

глаза

The eyes are blue.

# pieds

ноги

I have one pair of feet.

# des doigts

пальцы

The fingers are waving at us.

# pied

нога

My foot has five fingers.

# front

лоб

My brain is behind my forehead.

# cheveux

волосы

My hair is long and black.

# mains

руки

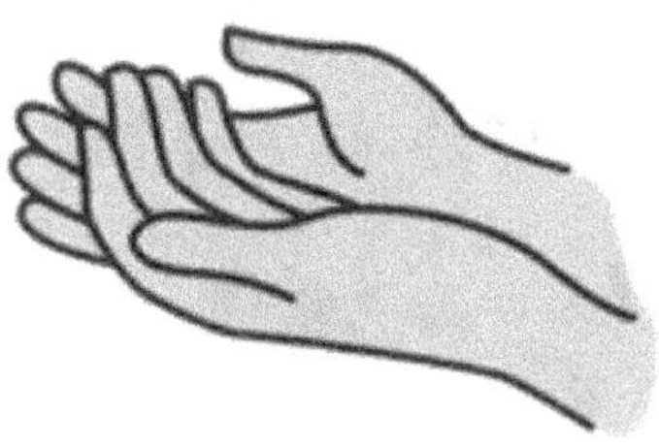

I will wash my hands in the sink.

# tête

глава

She has a big head.

# les hanches

бедра

The gorilla has his hands on his hips.

# les genoux

колени

She is begging on her knees.

# jambes

ноги

The tiger has strong legs.

# lèvres

губы

The lips have lipstick on.

# bouche

рот

He is covering his mouth with his hand.

# cou

шея

The necklace is very special to me.

# nez

нос

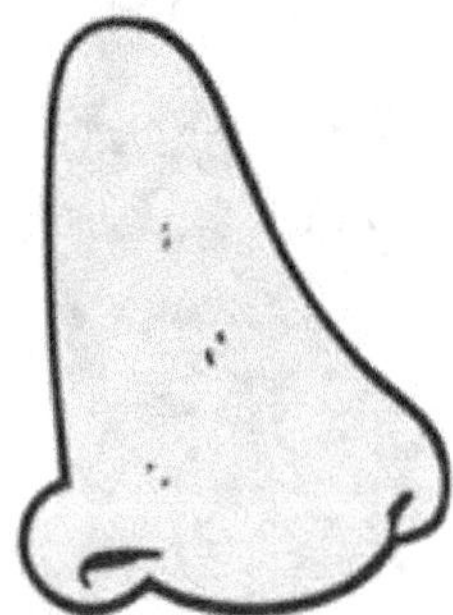

The nose smells something.

# épaules

плечи

He puts his hands on his shoulders.

# estomac

желудок

He has a big stomach.

# les dents

зубы

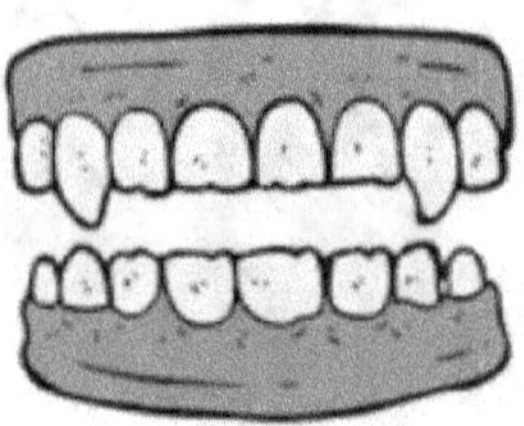

The teeth are clean and white.

# gorge

горло

He has a sore throat today.

# les orteils

пальцы на ногах

My toes are small.

# langue

язык

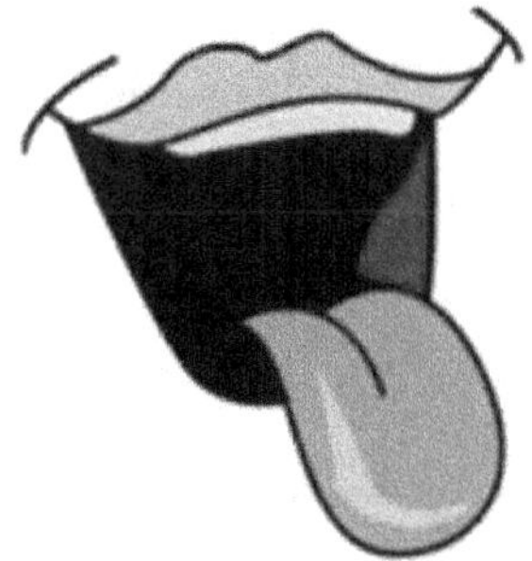

My tongue is licking ice cream.

# dent

зуб

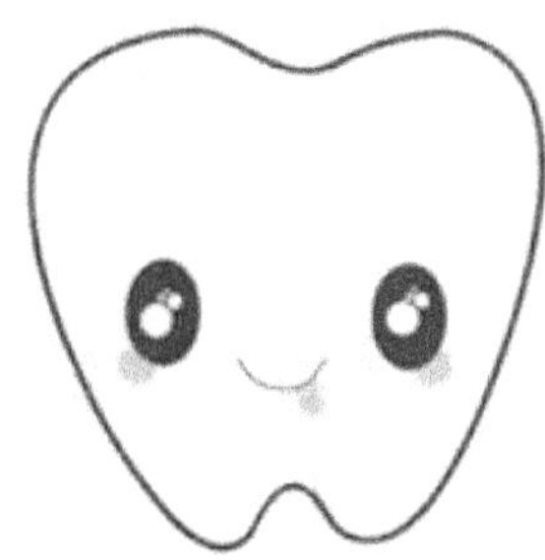

The tooth has big eyes.

# taille

талия

He has his hands on his waist.

# salopette

комбинезон

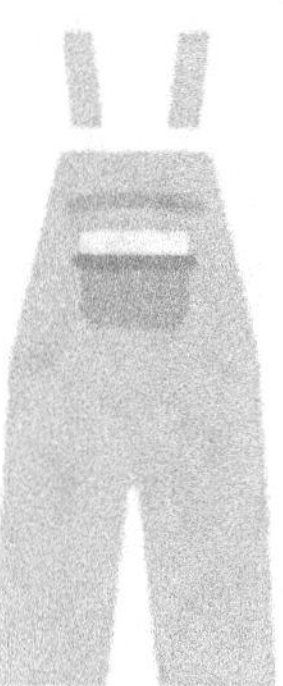

I bought these overalls for you!

# mitaines

рукавицы

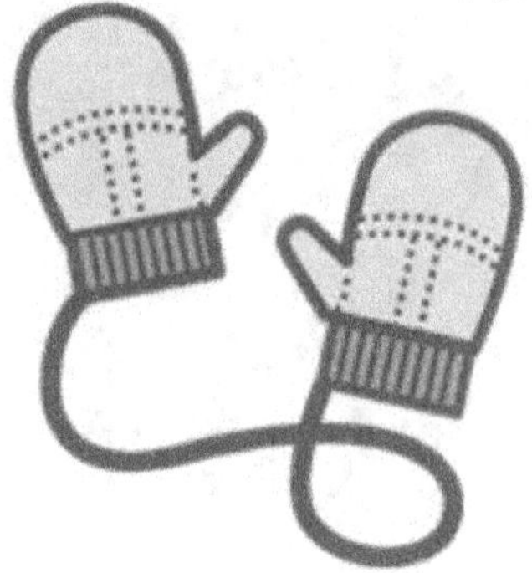

The mittens are very warm.

# bonnet

beanie

The beanie is for winter.

# tablier

фартук

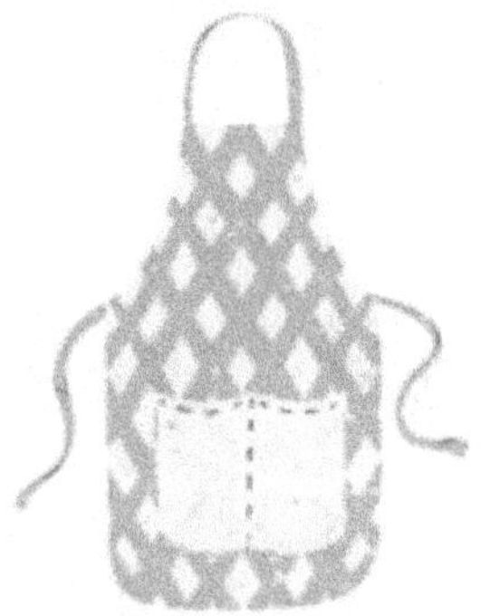

I wear my apron when I bake.

# poupée

кукла

The doll is for my baby sister.

# hochets

погремушки

The rattle is for the baby.

# jouet

игрушка

The toy is very fun.

# couche

подгузник

The baby has to wear a diaper.

# berceau

легкий шлем с забралом

She is sleeping in her bassinet.

# bavoir

нагрудник

My baby brother has to wear his
bib when he is eating.

# octogone

восьмиугольник

The octagon is saying okay!

# triangle

треугольник

The triangle has three corners.

# carré

квадрат

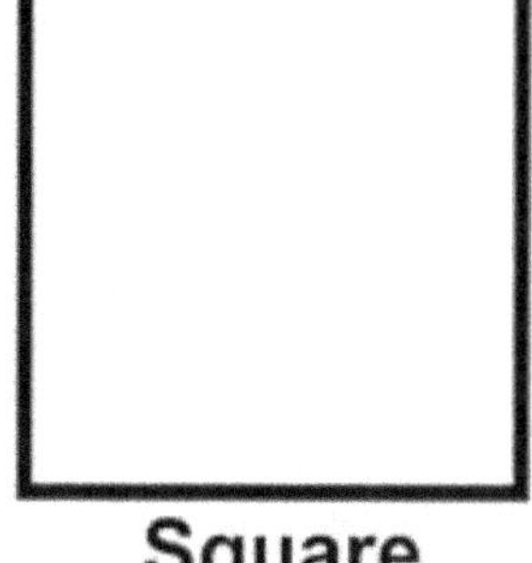

**Square**

The square has four sides.

# cercle

круг

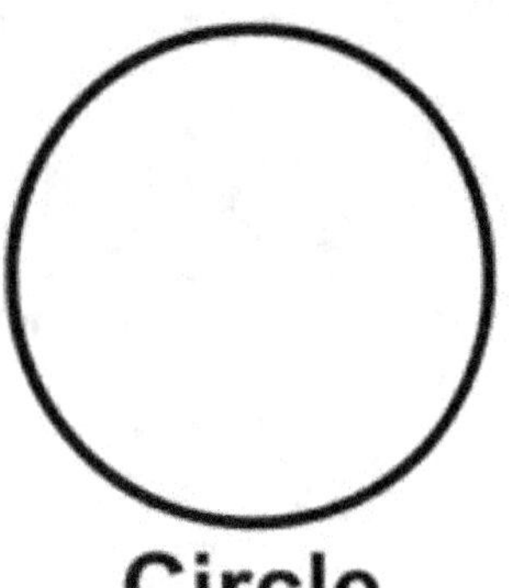

**Circle**

The circle is round.

# ovale

овальный

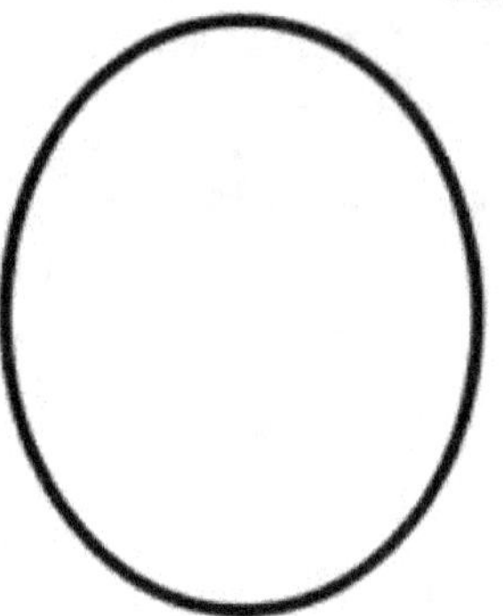

The oval shape looks like a circle.

# cœur

сердце

I drew a heart on my paper.

# traverser

пересекать

That sign is a cross.

# la flèche

стрелка

The arrow is pointing this way.

# cube

куб

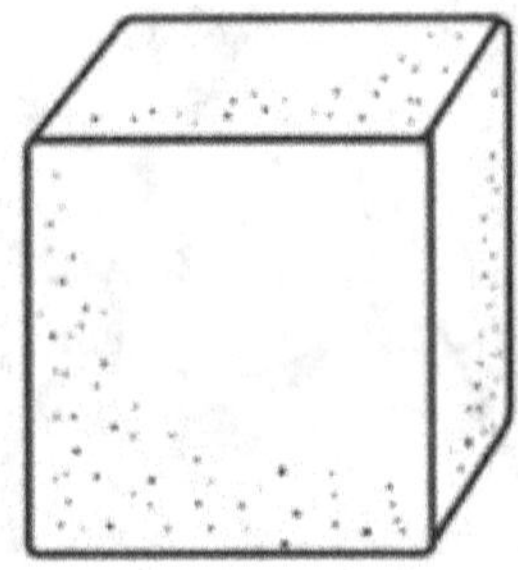

The cube is 3D.

# étoile

звезда

The star is yellow and shiny.

# tir à l'arc

стрельба из лука

The archery is where you aim.

# badminton

бадминтон

My favorite sport is badminton.

# criquet

крикет

I am very good at cricket.

# bowling

боулинг

I got one pin down at bowling!

# boxe

заниматься боксом

The boxing gloves are hot.

# tennis

большой теннис

He can hit the ball in tennis.

# faire de la planche a roulettes

скейтбординг

He skateboards to school.

# planche de surf

в серфинге

The shark loves surfing in the ocean.

# le hockey

хоккей

I like to play Ice hockey.

# yoga

йога

He is closing his eyes and doing yoga.

# épée

фехтование

They are fencing and dueling together.

# aptitude

фитнес

She will do some fitness in the pool.

# gymnastique

гимнастика

He can do brilliant gymnastics.

# karaté

каратэ

She is good at kicking in Karate.

# volley-ball

волейбол

She is holding a volleyball.

# musculation

гиревой спорт

The girl with brown hair can do weightlifting.

# basketball

баскетбол

He can balance the ball with one finger in basketball.

# base-ball

бейсбол

The little chick is in the finales at baseball.

# le rugby

регби

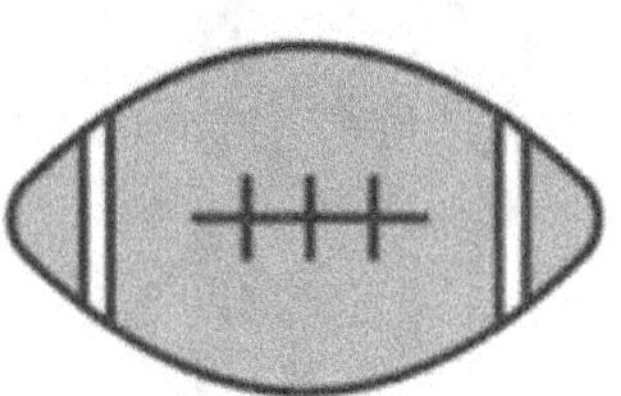

The rugby ball has white stripes.

# lutte

борьба

The sumo will compete in wrestling.

# course de voitures

автомобильная гонка

He is number one for car racing.

# cyclisme

катание на велосипеде

He is peacefully cycling on the road.

# fonctionnement

бег

He is running while listening to his earphones.

# tennis de table

настольный теннис

My brother and dad will play table tennis.

# pêche

рыбная ловля

He will go to the river to fish.

# judo

дзюдо

She has a red belt in Judo.

# escalade

альпинизм

He will climb the ladder.

# tournage

стрельба

He is shooting the archery board.

# le golf

гольф

She is going to compete in the golf competition.

# balade

поездка

He will ride his scooter.

# asseyez-vous

садиться

They are sitting down together.

# se lever

встаньте

She likes to stand up.

# bats toi

борьба

They are fighting over the book.

# rire

смех

He is laughing so hard!

# lis

читать

She read a picture book.

# jouer

играть

He went to play on the slide.

# ecoutez

слушать

He listened for the ice cream cart.

# pleurer

плач

He cried because he got a bad grade.

# pense

считать

He thought that the test would be hard.

# chanter

sing

He sang for the concert.

# regarder la télévision

смотри телевизор

He watched TV the whole night.

# danse

танец

She was a good dancer.

# allumer

включи

The light is turned on.

# éteindre

выключить

The light is turned off.

# gagner

выиграть

He won the contest.

# mouche

fly

The parrot can fly.

# couper

резать

He was cutting his nails.

# désinvolte

выбросить

He threw away the garbage.

# dormir

спать

He slept soundly.

# fermer

близко

He closed his mouth shut.

# ouvert

открыто

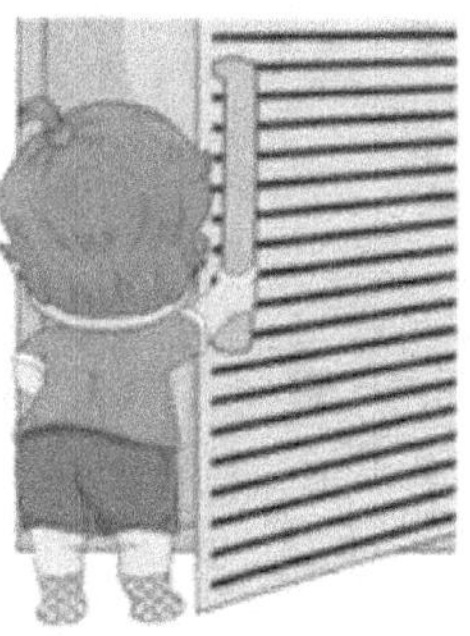

She opened the bathroom door.

# écrire

напишите

She wrote with a pencil.

# donner

дайте

Santa gave her a present.

# sauter

прыгать

She had fun jumping.

# manger

есть

The shark ate yummy ice cream.

# boisson

пить

The old British man drank tea.

# cuisinier

готовить

The microwave cooked his soup.

# lavage

мыть

You need to remember to wash your hands.

# attendre

подождите

He was waiting for the bus.

# montée

карабкаться

She climbed a lot of mountains.

# parler

разговаривать

Two best friends were talking together.

# crawl

ползать

The baby crawled on the floor.

# rêver

мечта

The Sloth dreamed about eating leaves.

# creuser

копать землю

That strong man dug a swimming pool.

# taper

хлопок

The baby clapped her hands.

# tricoter

вязать

She knits with the purple string.

# coudre

sew

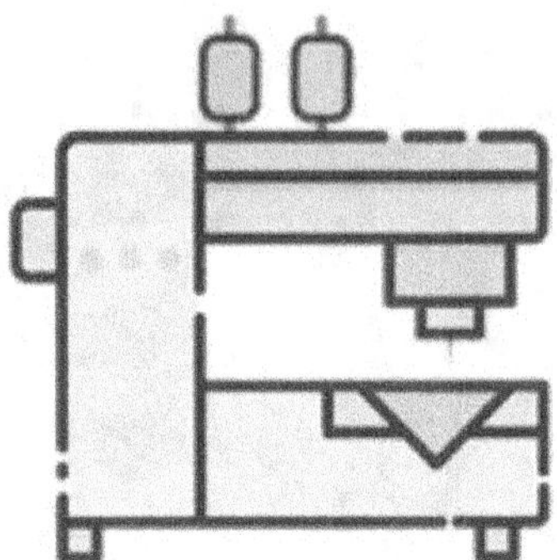

That is a sewing machine.

# odeur

запах

The perfume smelled great.

# baiser

поцелуй

He kissed his mother.

# étreinte

объятие

They hugged each other.

# ronfler

храп

The tiger snored.

# baigner

купать

He took a bath.

# s'incliner

поклонившись

He bowed to the judge.

# peindre

покрасить

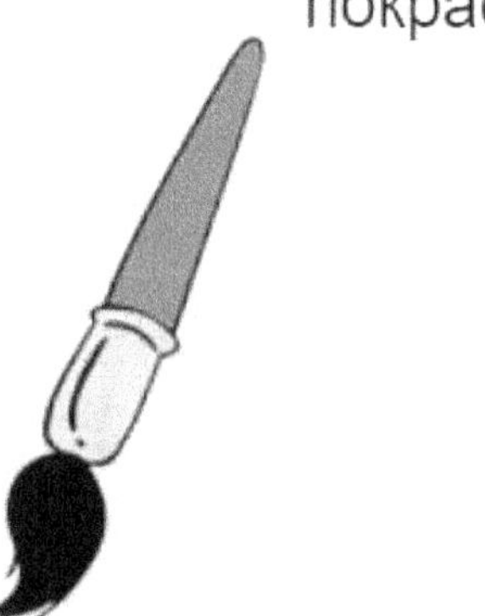

He painted a colorful picture.

# se plonger

пикирование

He dove to the deepest part of the ocean.

# ski

лыжа

The ski was expensive.

# empiler

стек

The books are stacked high.

# acheter

купить

They bought cereal.

# secouer

встряска

They shook hands together.

# programmeur

программист

He was a smart computer programmer.

# vétérinaire

ветеринар

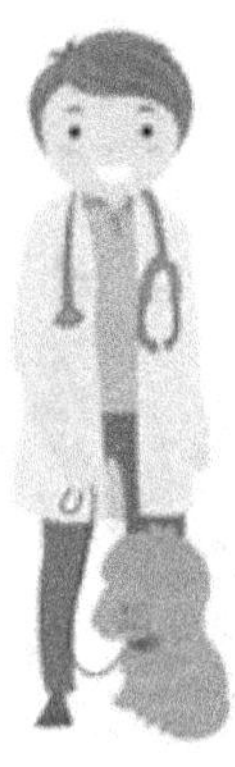

She is a veterinarian.

# vendeur de rue

уличный торговец

That street vendor sells hot dogs.

# mineur

шахтер

That Miner will find gold.

# prof

учитель

The owl is the teacher.

# groom

коридорный

That Bellboy is fat.

# orateur

оратор

The chicken is a great Speaker.

# boucher

мясник

The Butcher sells fish.

# pharmacien

фармацевт

That Pharmacist saved a person's life.

# réceptionniste

портье

He is a Receptionist.

# politicien

политик

He wants to be a Politician.

# guide touristique

туристический гид

That Tour guide led us around Japan.

# entrepreneur

предприниматель

He is an Entrepreneur.

# danseuse de ballet

балерина

She is training to be a Ballet dancer.

# astronaute

астронавт

He is a great astronaut.

# juge

судья

That Judge is always fair.

# avocat

адвокат

The lawyer is serious.

# la caissière

касса

She is a cashier at the market.

# conducteur de taxi

таксист

He is a fast Taxi driver.

# plombier

водопроводчик

That Plumber fixes toilets.

# musicien

музыкант

She wants to be a Musician like her teacher.

# chef

шеф-повар

The chef makes fast food.

# boulanger

пекарь

That baker is a bread.

# artiste

художник

That Artist came from Italy.

# acteur

актер

That actor is famous.

# barman

бармен

The Bartender works in a bar.

# coiffeur

парикмахер

That girl is a Hairdresser.

# évêques

епископы

He is a Bishop.

# opticien

оптик

She went to an Optician.

# fleuriste

флорист

She is a great Florist.

# écrivain

писатель

He is a famous author.

# comptable

бухгалтер

My accountant is loyal.

# du vin

вино

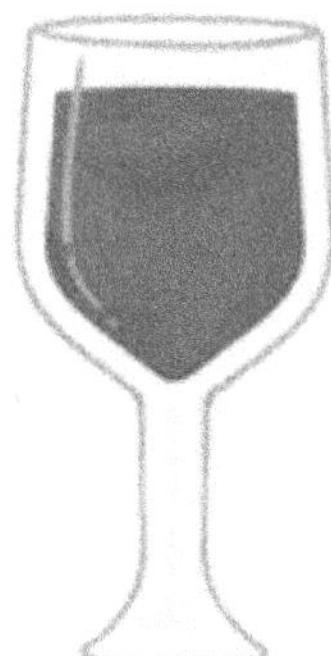

That wine tastes good.

# café

кофе

That coffee is bitter.

# limonade

лимонад

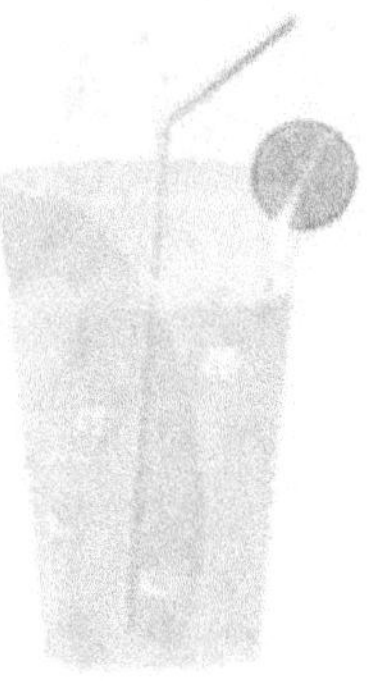

The lemonade is refreshing.

# chocolat chaud

горячий шоколад

I drink hot chocolate every day.

# milk-shake

молочный коктейль

The milkshake has whipped cream.

# eau

вода

The water is not cold.

# thé

чай

The tea is hot.

# lait

молоко

Milk is white.

# bière

пиво

The beer is foamy.

# un soda

содовый

The soda is fizzy.

# smoothie

льстец

The smoothie is a watermelon flavor.

# milk-shake

молочный коктейль

The milkshake has whipped cream.

# lait de coco

кокосовое молоко

The coconut milk is yummy.

# du jus d'orange

апельсиновый сок

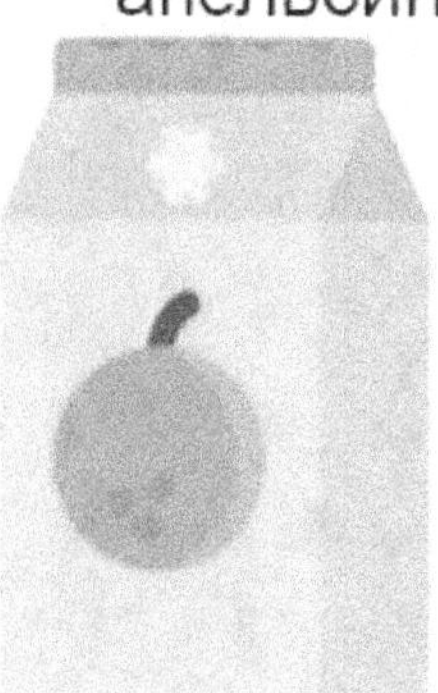

The orange juice is made from oranges.

# cacao

какао

The cocoa is sweet.

# fromage

сыр

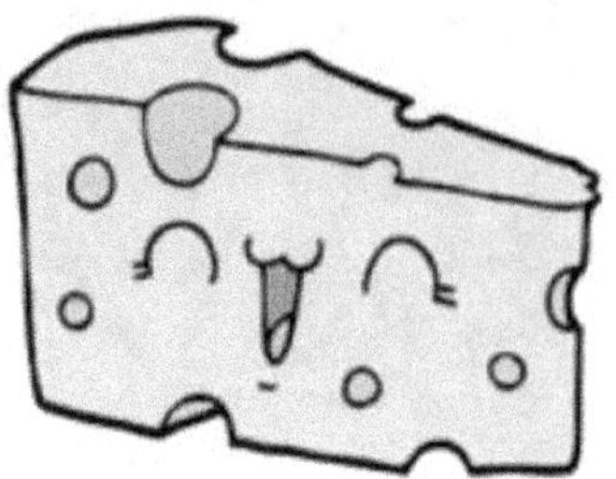

The cheese is creamy.

# oeuf

яйцо

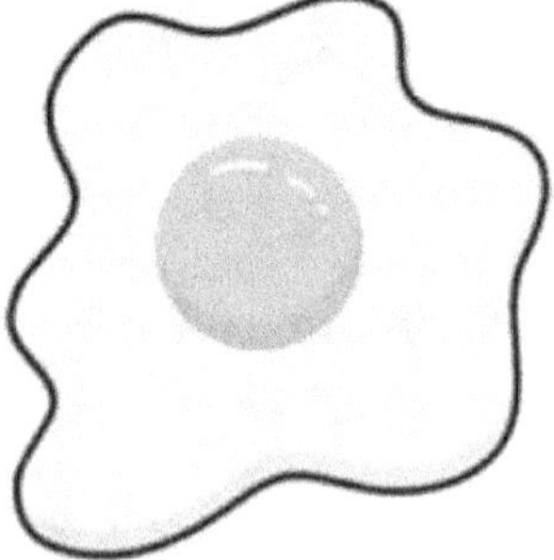

The egg is fried.

# beurre

сливочное масло

The butter is put on bread.

# margarine

маргарин

Margarine looks like butter.

# yaourt

йогурт

That yogurt is popular.

# cottage cheese

творог

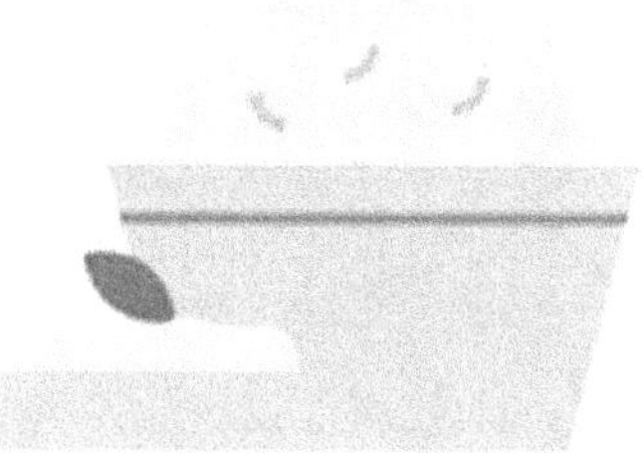

The cottage cheese is put on crackers.

# crème glacée

мороженое

They have a triple scoop ice cream.

# crème

пломбир

That is a lot of creams.

# sandwich

сандвич

That sandwich is healthy.

# saucisse

колбаса

Americans love sausages.

# hamburger

гамбургер

That hamburger looks happy.

# hot-dog

хот-дог

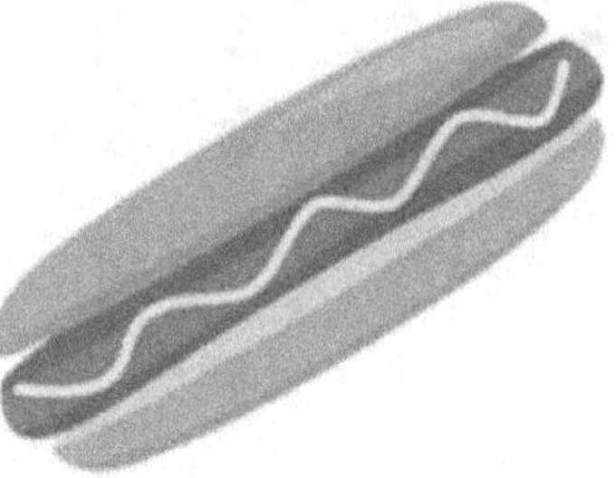

That hot dog has mustard on it.

# pain

хлеб

That bread is saying hello.

# pizza

пицца

That pizza is cheesy.

# steak

стейк

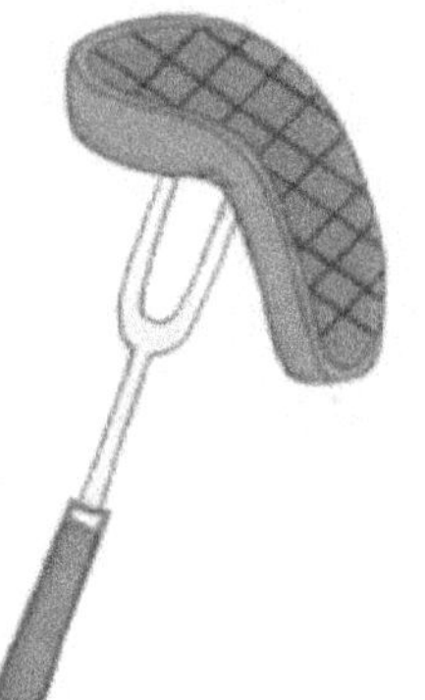

The steak was grilled.

# poulet rôti

жареный цыпленок

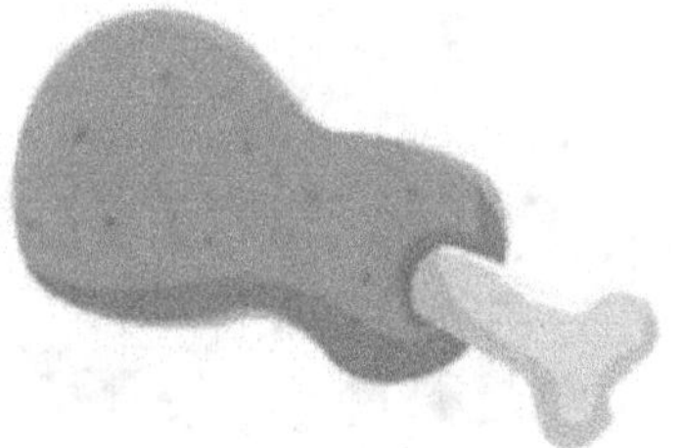

Roast Chicken is delicious.

# poisson

рыбы

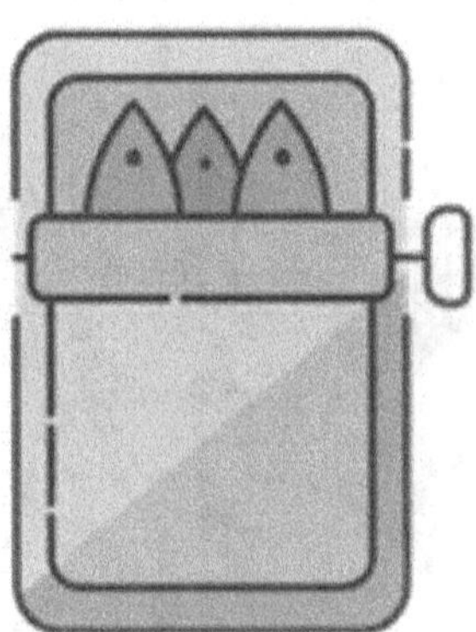

You can buy canned fish in the market.

# fruit de mer

морепродукты

Lobster is expensive seafood.

# jambon

ветчина

Ham can be put in sandwiches.

# kebab

кебаб

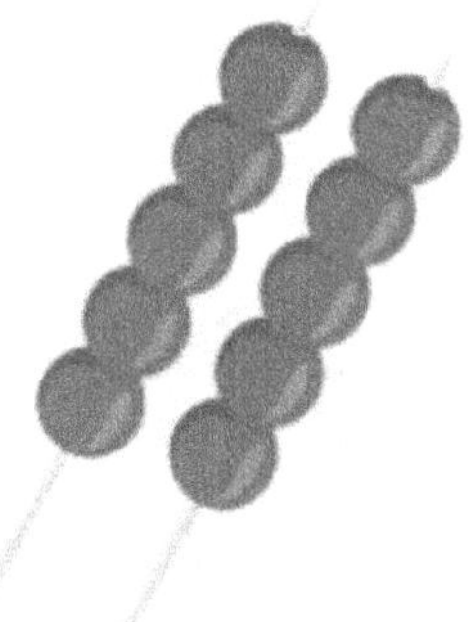

Kebab is a delicacy in America.

# bacon

бекон

That bacon is smiling.

# crème fraîche

сметана

You can dip your chips in sour cream.

# vache

корова

Cows are black and white.

# lapin

кролик

That rabbit is fun to play with.

# canard

утка

That duck is content.

# crevette

креветка

The shrimp has six legs.

# porc

свинья

That pig is pink and fat.

# abeille

пчелка

The bee has a stinger.

# chèvre

козел

That goat has a white horn.

# crabe

краб

The crab has two big pincers.

# cerf

олень

That deer is sleeping.

# dinde

турция

The turkey has a giant tail.

# colombe

голубка

That dove is carrying a plant.

# mouton

овец

That sheep has fluffy wool.

# poisson

рыбы

That fish has colorful fins.

# poulet

курица

That chicken is waking everybody up.

# cheval

лошадь

The horse has a red mane.

# chaise

стул

That wing chair is yellow.

# meuble tv

тумба под тв

The TV stand can hold books.

# canapé

диван

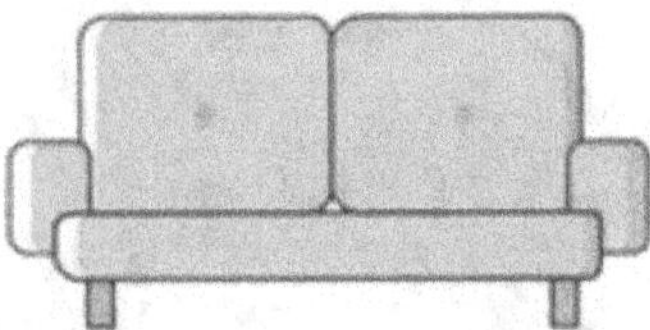

The sofa is comfortable to sit on.

# coussins

cushions

The cushion helps soften your seat.

# téléphone

телефон

The telephone is ringing.

# télévision

телевидение

That television is big.

# haut-parleurs

динамики

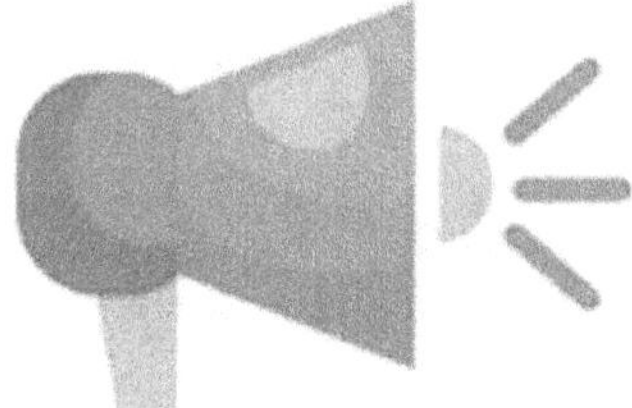

That speaker is used to increase the volume.

# table d'appoint

столик

That end table is sparkling clean.

# service à thé

чайный сервиз

That tea set is from China.

# cheminée

камин

The fireplace makes me warm.

# télécommandes

remotes

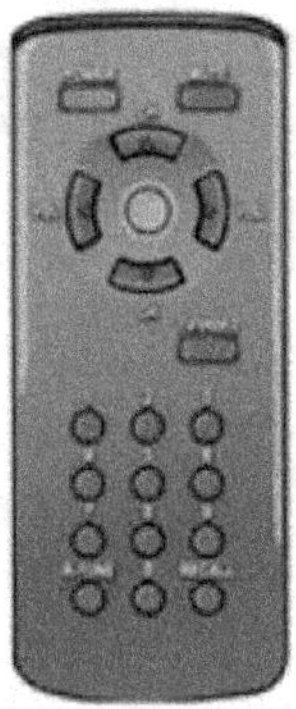

The remote has lots of buttons.

# ventilateur électrique

электрический вентилятор

The fan is blowing wind.

# lampadaire

торшер

The floor lamp is very tall.

# tapis

ковер

The carpet is soft and silky.

# bureaux

парты

The table is made of wood.

# stores

шторы

I will pull the blinds down.

# rideaux

шторы

She opened the curtains.

# image

картина

The picture is about the mountains and the sky.

# vase

ваза

The roses are all in a vase.

# l'horloge

часы

The alarm clock is beeping.

# oreiller

подушка

The pillow is pink and yellow.

# cintre

вешалка для шляп

The hat stand has only one hat on it.

# mettre la table

туалетный столик

I have made up on my dressing table.

# lampe de table

настольная лампа

The table lamp will help me see in the dark.

# miroir

зеркало

The mirror is very tall.

# planche a repasser

гладильная доска

Don't touch the ironing board, it's hot!

# boîte avec tiroir

коробка с ящиком

You can keep your clothes in the hope chest.

# table de chevet

прикроватный столик

The nightstand has my lamp on it.

# lit

постель

The bed is charming.

# climatisation

кондиционер

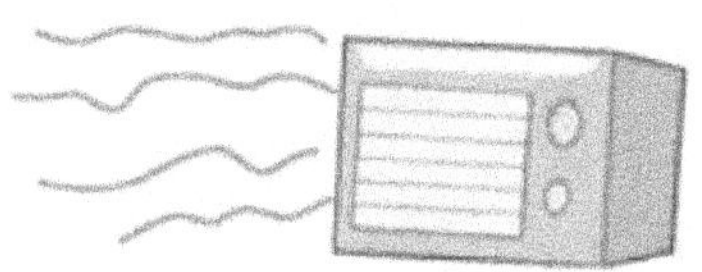

The air conditioner is cold.

# cruche

кувшин

The measuring jug has nothing inside.

# dentifrice

зубная паста

The toothpaste is mint flavored.

# brosse à dents

зубная щетка

The toothbrush has toothpaste on it.

# savon

мыло

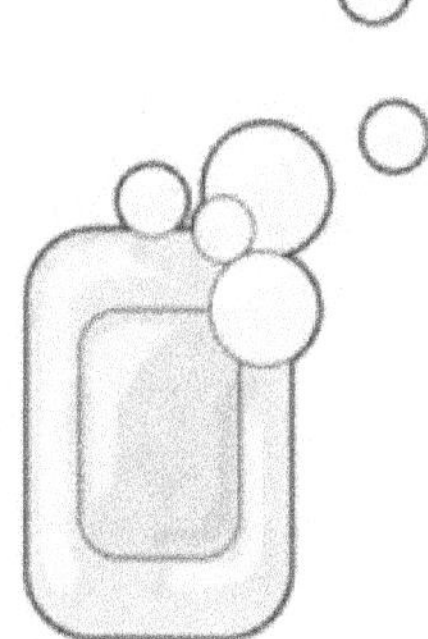

The soap is very bubbly.

# pince à linge

прищепки

The clothespin will clip my clothes.

# cintre

вешалка

The hanger is hanging my boots.

# sèche-cheveux

фен

The hairdryer will blow my hair.

# shampooing

шампунь

The shampoo is used to clean your hair.

# bulle

пузырь

The bubbles are very fun to play in.

# brosse

щетка

She is brushing her hair with the brush.

## papier toilette

туалетная бумага

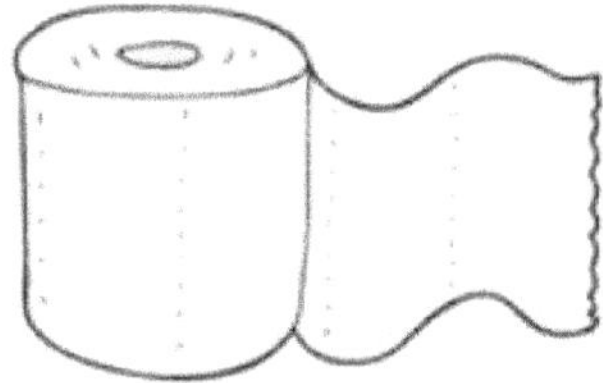

The toilet paper is used to dry your hands.

## serviette

полотенце

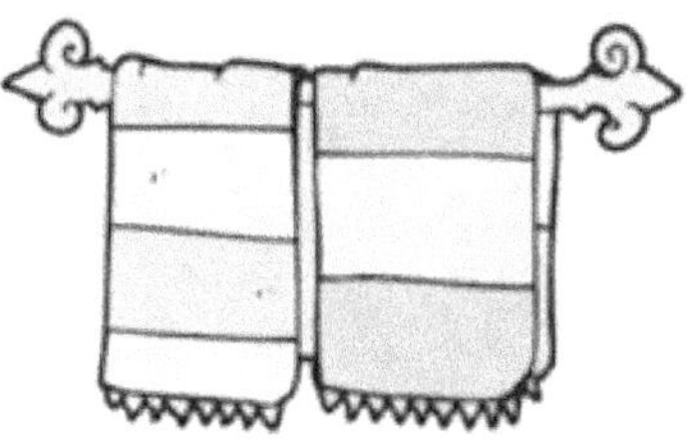

We have two towels on the rack.

## corde à linge

велогонка

My shirt is hanging on the clothesline.

## douche

душ

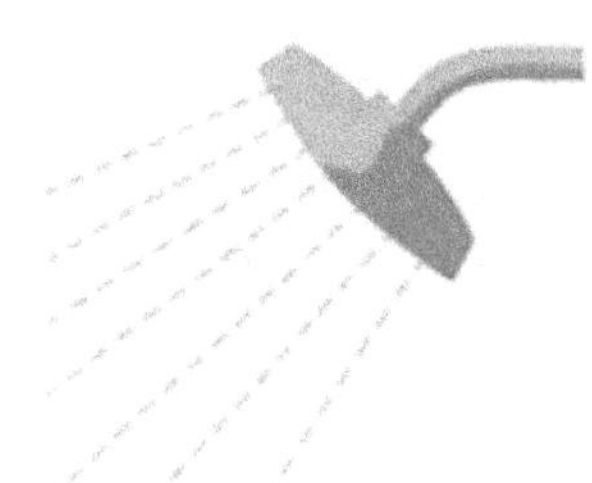

The shower is spraying water.

## baignoire

ванна

The bathtub is comfortable.

## lessive

стиральный порошок

The laundry detergent is used with the washing machine.

# seau

ведро

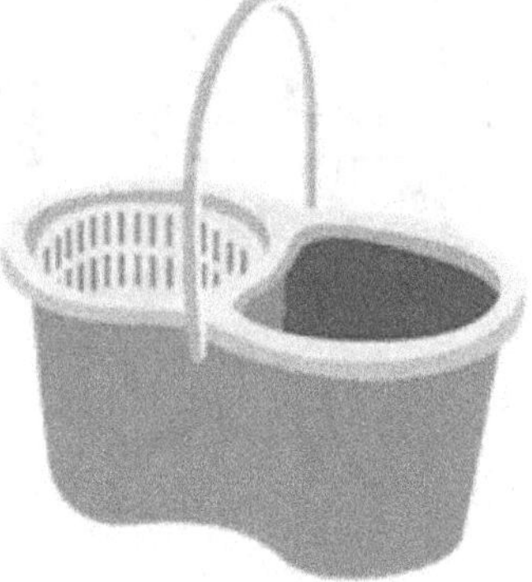

Can you help me fill up the bucket?

# vadrouilles

швабры

The mop is used for mopping the floor.

# savon liquide

жидкое мыло

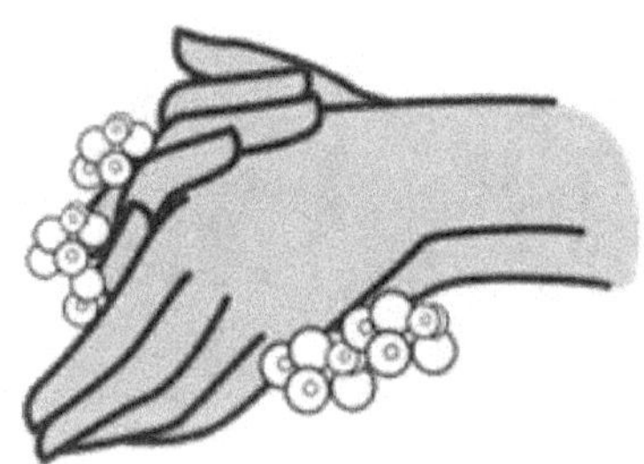

I use soapy water to wash my hands.

# lessive en poudre

стиральный порошок

I will scoop up the washing powder.

# sac poubelle

мусорная корзина

The trash bag is full of trash.

# poubelle

мусорный ящик

You have only to put recylcle trash in the trash can.

# les puits

раковины

You should wash your hands in the sink.

# cuvette des toilettes

унитаз

She let her bunny use the toilet.

# machine à laver

стиральная машина

The washing machine wash your clothes.

# panier à linge

корзина для белья

She is putting all the clothes into the laundry basket.

# le rasoir

бритва

He uses the razor to shave his beard.

# rasoir électrique

электробритва

The electric razor works faster than the normal one.

# crème à raser

крем для бритья

The shaving cream is fluffy.

# bain de bouche

полоскание для рта

The mouthwash smells very lovely.

# coton-tige

ватный тампон

Q-tip can be used for many things.

# brosse à cheveux

щетка для волос

She brushes her hair with her hairbrush.

# peigne

расческа

Her dad will comb her hair for her.

# nettoyant

очищающее средство

Put the cap back on the cleanser bottle.

# échelle

масштаб

You can measure things on the scale.

# papier de soie

бумажные салфетки

The tissue is on the counter.

# jouets de bain

игрушки для ванной

The little duck is a bath toy.

# robinet

кран

The faucet is broken.

# miroir

зеркало

He is looking in the mirror.

# tapis de bain

коврик для ванной

The bath mat is purple and yellow.